WORKING PAPERS TO ACCOMPANY

ADVANCED ACCOUNTING

Fifth Edition

Andrew A. Haried, PhD, CPA
Professor of Accounting
Arizona State University

Leroy F. Imdieke, PhD, CPA
Professor of Accounting
Arizona State University

Ralph E. Smith, PhD, CPA
Professor of Accounting
Arizona State University

John Wiley & Sons, Inc.
New York / Chichester / Brisbane / Toronto / Singapore

ISBN 0 471 53332 7

Printed in the United States of America

10 9 8 7 6 5 4 3 2 1

WORKING PAPERS
TO ACCOMPANY

ADVANCED ACCOUNTING

Fifth Edition

NAME

SECTION

DATE

P COMPANY AND SUBSIDIARY
Consolidated Balance Sheet Workpaper
November 30, 1992

	P Company	S Company	Eliminations Debit	Eliminations Credit	Consolidated Balances
I.					
Current Assets	880000	240000			
Investment in S Company	160000				
Long-term Assets	1400000	400000			
Other Assets	90000	40000			
Total	2530000	680000			
Current Liabilities	640000	270000			
Long-term Liabilities	850000	290000			
Common Stock:					
P Company	600000				
S Company		160000			
Retained Earnings					
P Company	440000				
S Company		(400000)			
Total	2530000	680000			
II.					
Current Assets	780000	280000			
Investment in S Company	160000				
Long-term Assets	1200000	400000			
Other Assets	70000	50000			
Total	2210000	730000			

	P Company	S Company	Eliminations Debit	Eliminations Credit	Consolidated Balances
Current Liabilities	670000	260000			
Long-term Liabilities	920000	270000			
Common Stock:					
P Company	600000				
S Company		160000			
Retained Earnings					
P Company	20000				
S Company		400000			
Total	2210000	730000			

NAME

SECTION

DATE

PERCY COMPANY AND SUBSIDIARY
Consolidated Balance Sheet Workpaper
January 1, 1992

	Percy Company	Ship Company	Eliminations Debit	Eliminations Credit	Consolidated Balances
Cash	41000	24000			
Accounts receivable	48000	19000			
Inventory	39000	17000			
Investment in Ship	110000				
Plant Assets	132000	68500			
Accumulated depreciation	(42000)	(14500)			
Total	328000	114000			
Current liabilities	15500	23000			
Mortgage notes payable	30000				
Common stock:					
Percy Company	180000				
Ship Company		60000			
Premium on common stock:					
Percy Company	60000				
Ship Company		11000			
Retained earnings:					
Percy Company	42500				
Ship Company		20000			
Total	328000	114000			

NAME

SECTION

DATE

P COMPANY AND SUBSIDIARY
Consolidated Balance Sheet Workpaper
August 1, 1992

	P Company	S Company	Eliminations Debit	Eliminations Credit	Consolidated Balances
Cash	179200	86000			
Receivables	36000	126000			
Inventory	268000	108000			
Investment in Bonds	306000				
Investment in S Company Stock	535800				
Plant and Equipment	573000	320000			
Land	200000	280000			
Total	2428000	920000			
Accounts Payable	174000	78000			
Accrued Expenses	32400	26000			
Bonds Payable, 8%		200000			
Common Stock:					
P Company	1500000				
S Company		400000			
Other Contributed Capital:					
P Company	240000				
S Company		60000			
Retained Earnings:					
P Company	481600				
S Company		156000			
Total	2428000	920000			
Advances from P Company					

NAME _____

SECTION _____

DATE _____

POOL COMPANY AND SUBSIDIARIES
Consolidated Balance Sheet Workpaper
January 2, 1992

	Pool Company	Swamp Company	Troy Company	Eliminations Debit	Eliminations Credit	Consolidated Balances
Cash	3000	15760	20000			
Accounts receivable	48000	24000	20000			
Note receivable		8000				
Interest receivable		240				
Inventory	120000	96000	56000			
Investment in Swamp Company	232000					
Investment in Troy Company	145000					
Equipment	60000	40000	30000			
Land	140000	80000	70000			
Total	748000	264000	196000			

NAME _____

SECTION _____

DATE _____

	Play Company	Shark Company	Renee Company	Eliminations Debit	Eliminations Credit	Consolidated Balances
Accounts payable	2 5 5 0 0	2 0 0 0 0	1 0 5 0 0			
Income tax payable	3 0 0 0 0	8 0 0 0				
Notes payable		6 0 0 0	9 0 0 0			
Bonds payable	1 0 0 0 0 0					
Common stock:						
Play Company	3 6 3 0 0 0					
Shark Company		1 4 4 0 0 0				
Renee Company			4 2 0 0 0			
Other contributed capital:						
Play Company	1 7 0 6 0 0					
Shark Company		1 2 0 0 0				
Renee Company			3 0 0 0 0			
Retained earnings:						
Play Company	1 4 9 0 0 0					
Shark Company		4 5 0 0				
Renee Company			(1 0 0 0 0)			
Total	8 3 8 1 0 0	1 9 4 5 0 0	8 1 5 0 0			

NAME

SECTION

DATE

PEACE COMPANY AND SUBSIDIARY
Consolidated Balance Sheet Workpaper
January 1, 1992

	Peace Company	Shaw Company	Eliminations Debit	Eliminations Credit	Consolidated Balances
Cash	2800000	150000			
Accounts receivable	480000	425000			
Note receivable	100000	- 0 -			
Inventory	2200000	1200000			
Investment in Shaw Company	4875000	- 0 -			
Plant and equipment	6365000	3400000			
Land	1700000	825000			
Total	16000000	6000000			
Accounts payable	350000	250000			
Notes payable	2500000	100000			
Common stock:					
Peace Company	5760000				
Shaw Company		4880000			
Other contributed capital:					
Peace Company	3840000				
Shaw Company		1220000			
Treasury Stock Held					
Shaw Company		(1200000)			
Retained Earnings:					
Peace Company	3550000				
Shaw Company		750000			
Total	16000000	6000000			

NAME

SECTION

DATE

PET COMPANY AND SUBSIDIARY
Consolidated Statements Workpaper
For the Year Ended December 31, 1992

	Pet Company	Sable Company	Eliminations Debit	Eliminations Credit	Consolidated Balances
INCOME STATEMENT					
Sales	3120000	1545000			
Dividend Income	2000				
Total Revenue	3140000	1545000			
Cost of Goods Sold	2000000	1215000			
Other Expense	455000	295000			
Total Cost and Expense	2455000	1510000			
Net Income to Retained Earnings	685000	35000			
RETAINED EARNINGS STATEMENT					
1/1 Retained Earnings - Pet	760000				
- Sable		240000			
Net Income from Above	685000	35000			
Dividends Declared - Pet	(175000)				
- Sable		(20000)			
12/31 Retained Earnings to Balance Sheet	1270000	255000			

	Pet Company	Sable Company	Eliminations		Consolidated Balances
			Debit	Credit	
BALANCE SHEET					
Cash	59500	29000			
Accounts Receivable	41000	42000			
Inventory	49500	36500			
Investment in Sable Company	120000				
Land	4000	12000			
Total	274000	119500			
Accounts Payable	27000	14000			
Common Stock - Pet	120000				
- Sable		80000			
Retained Earnings from Above	127000	25500			
Total	274000	119500			

NAME

SECTION

DATE

PRIME COMPANY AND SUBSIDIARY
Consolidated Statements Workpaper
For the Year Ended December 31, 1992

	Prime Company	Smart Company	Eliminations Debit	Eliminations Credit	Consolidated Balances
INCOME STATEMENT					
Sales	380000	150000			
Dividend Income	10000				
Total Revenue	390000	150000			
Cost of Goods Sold	225000	62500			
Other Expense	50000	40000			
Total Cost and Expense	275000	102500			
Net Income to Retained Earnings	115000	47500			
RETAINED EARNINGS STATEMENT					
1/1 Retained Earnings - Prime	250000				
- Smart		40000			
Net Income from Above	115000	47500			
Dividends Declared - Prime	(15000)				
- Smart		(10000)			
12/31 Retained Earnings to Balance Sheet	125000	77500			

NAME _____

SECTION _____

DATE _____

BALANCE SHEET	Prime Company	Smart Company	Eliminations Debit	Eliminations Credit	Consolidated Balances
Cash	25000	30000			
Inventory	105000	97500			
Investment in Smart Company	145000				
Land	37500	60000			
Total	312500	187500			
Accounts Payable	72500	17500			
Capital Stock - Prime	100000				
- Smart		75000			
Other Contributed Capital - Prime	15000				
- Smart		17500			
Retained Earnings from Above	125000	77500			
Total	312500	187500			

NAME _____

SECTION _____

DATE _____

PEACE COMPANY AND SUBSIDIARY
Consolidated Statements Workpaper
For the Year Ended December 31, 1992

	Peace Company	Shaw Company	Eliminations Debit	Eliminations Credit	Minority Interest	Consolidated Balances
INCOME STATEMENT						
Sales	549120	292580				
Dividend Income	16000					
Total Revenue	565120	292580				
Cost of Goods Sold:						
Inventory, 1/1	69360	19680				
Purchases	303000	162800				
	372360	182480				
Inventory, 12/31	22520	12300				
Cost of Goods Sold	349840	170180				
Selling Expense	37082	19334				
Other Expense	14888	12796				
Total Cost and Expense	401810	202310				
Net/Combined Income	163310	90270				
Minority Interest in Income						
Net Income to Retained Earnings	163310	90270				
RETAINED EARNINGS STATEMENT						
1/1 Retained Earnings:						
Peace Company	222352					
Shaw Company		134998				
Net Income from Above	163310	90270				
Dividends Declared						
Peace Company	(30000)					
Shaw Company		(20000)				
12/31 Retained Earnings to Bal. Sheet	355662	205268				

	Peace Company	Shaw Company	Eliminations		Minority Interest	Consolidated Balances
			Debit	Credit		
BALANCE SHEET						
Cash	6 2 8 1 6	6 8 0 0 0				
Accounts and Notes Receivable	2 1 6 0 0 0	2 0 8 5 2 0				
Inventories	2 2 5 2 0	1 2 3 0 0				
Investment in Peace Company	3 8 0 0 0 0					
Plant Assets	3 0 1 6 0 4	2 1 3 2 7 4				
Total	9 8 2 9 4 0	5 0 2 0 9 4				
Accounts and Notes Payable	8 4 4 7 8	3 2 5 4 0				
Other Liabilities	4 2 8 0 0	1 4 2 8 6				
Common Stock						
Peace Company	2 0 0 0 0 0					
Shaw Company		1 0 0 0 0 0				
Premium on Common Stock						
Peace Company	3 0 0 0 0 0					
Shaw Company		1 5 0 0 0 0				
Retained Earnings from Above	3 5 5 6 6 2	2 0 5 2 6 8				
Minority Interest in Net Assets						
Total	9 8 2 9 4 0	5 0 2 0 9 4				

NAME

SECTION

DATE

PAIR COMPANY AND SUBSIDIARY
Consolidated Statements Workpaper
For the Year Ended December 31, 1992

	Pair Company	Snap Company	Eliminations Debit	Eliminations Credit	Minority Interest	Consolidated Balances
INCOME STATEMENT						
Sales	9 6 0 0 0 0	4 2 0 0 0 0				
Dividend Income	8 0 0 0					
Total Revenue	1 0 4 0 0 0 0	4 2 0 0 0 0				
Cost of Goods Sold						
Inventory, 1/1	1 4 0 0 0 0	8 0 0 0 0				
Purchases	8 4 0 0 0 0	2 0 0 0 0 0				
	9 8 0 0 0 0	2 8 0 0 0 0				
Inventory, 12/31	2 0 0 0 0 0	1 0 0 0 0 0				
Cost of Goods Sold	7 8 0 0 0 0	1 8 0 0 0 0				
Other Expense	1 0 0 0 0 0	8 0 0 0 0				
Total Cost and Expense	8 8 0 0 0 0	2 6 0 0 0 0				
Net/Combined Income	1 6 0 0 0 0	1 6 0 0 0 0				
Minority Interest in Income						
Net Income to Retained Earnings	1 6 0 0 0 0	1 6 0 0 0 0				
RETAINED EARNINGS STATEMENT						
1/1 Retained Earnings:						
Pair Company	4 0 0 0 0 0					
Snap Company		2 0 0 0 0 0				
Net Income from Above	1 6 0 0 0 0	1 6 0 0 0 0				
Dividends Declared:						
Pair Company	(1 0 0 0 0 0)					
Snap Company		(1 0 0 0 0 0)				
12/31 Retained Earnings to Balance Sheet	4 6 0 0 0 0	2 6 0 0 0 0				

	Pair Company	Snap Company	Eliminations Debit	Eliminations Credit	Minority Interest	Consolidated Balances
BALANCE SHEET						
Cash	8 0 0 0	1 4 0 0 0				
Account Receivable	2 2 0 0 0	1 6 0 0 0				
Inventory, 12/31	2 0 0 0 0	1 0 0 0 0				
Advance to Snap Company	4 0 0 0					
Investment in Snap Company	5 0 0 0 0					
Plant and Equipment	5 0 0 0 0	4 0 0 0 0				
Land	8 0 0 0	6 0 0 0				
Total	1 6 2 0 0 0	8 6 0 0 0				
Accounts Payable	6 0 0 0	6 0 0 0				
Other Liabilities	1 0 0 0 0					
Advances from Pair Company		4 0 0 0				
Capital Stock:						
Pair Company	1 0 0 0 0 0					
Snap Company		5 0 0 0 0				
Retained Earnings from Above	4 6 0 0 0	2 6 0 0 0				
Minority Interest in Net Assets						
Total	1 6 2 0 0 0	8 6 0 0 0				

NAME

SECTION

DATE

POOR COMPANY AND SUBSIDIARY
Consolidated Statements Workpaper
For the Year Ended December 31, 1992

	Poor Company	Sob Company	Eliminations Debit	Eliminations Credit	Minority Interest	Consolidated Balances
INCOME STATEMENT						
Sales	105000	40000				
Dividend Income	4000					
Total Revenue	109000	40000				
Cost of Goods Sold	90000	20000				
Other Expense	10000	7000				
Total Cost and Expense	100000	27000				
Net/Combined Income	9000	13000				
Minority Interest in Income						
Net Income to Retained Earnings	9000	13000				
RETAINED EARNINGS STATEMENT						
Retained Earnings, 1/1:						
Poor Company	20000					
Sob Company		5000				
Net Income from Above	9000	13000				
Dividends Declared:						
Poor Company	(10000)					
Sob Company		(5000)				
12/31 Retained Earnings to Balance Sheet	19000	13000				

BALANCE SHEET	Poor Company	Sob Company	Eliminations Debit	Eliminations Credit	Minority Interest	Consolidated Balances
Cash	1 3 0 0 0	6 7 5 0				
Accounts Receivable	2 1 0 0 0	1 7 0 0 0				
Inventory	1 5 0 0 0	8 0 0 0				
Investment in Sob Company	4 8 0 0 0					
Land	5 2 0 0 0	4 8 0 0 0				
Total	1 4 9 0 0 0	7 9 7 5 0				
Accounts Payable	5 0 0 0	6 0 0 0				
Other Liabilities	5 0 0 0	4 0 0 0				
Capital Stock:						
Poor Company	1 0 0 0 0 0					
Sob Company		5 1 7 5 0				
Other Contributed Capital:						
Poor Company	2 0 0 0 0					
Sob Company		5 0 0 0				
Retained Earnings from Above	1 9 0 0 0	1 3 0 0 0				
Minority Interest in Net Assets						
Total	1 4 9 0 0 0	7 9 7 5 0				

NAME

SECTION

DATE

PLACER COMPANY AND SUBSIDIARY
Consolidated Statements Workpaper
For the Year Ended December 31, 1992

	Placer Company	Sands Company	Eliminations Debit	Eliminations Credit	Minority Interest	Consolidated Balances
INCOME STATEMENT						
Sales	1 344 000	500 000				
Dividend and Interest Income	56 000	- 0 -				
Total Revenue	1 400 000	500 000				
Cost of Goods Sold	822 000	263 000				
Operating Expenses	268 000	124 000				
Total Cost and Expense	1 090 000	387 000				
Net/Combined Income	310 000	113 000				
Minority Interest in Income						
Net Income to Retained Earnings	310 000	113 000				
RETAINED EARNINGS STATEMENT						
1/1 Retained Earnings:						
Placer Company	662 000					
Sands Company		217 000				
Net Income from Above	310 000	113 000				
Dividends Declared:						
Placer Company	(70 000)					
Sands Company		(60 000)				
12/31 Retained Earnings to Balance Sheet	920 000	270 000				

NAME _____

SECTION _____

DATE _____

BALANCE SHEET	Plumb Company	Strap Company	Eliminations Debit	Eliminations Credit	Minority Interest	Consolidated Balances
Cash	5 7 5 0 0	6 0 0 0 0				
Inventory	2 1 0 0 0 0	1 9 5 0 0 0				
Investment in Strap Company	3 5 7 5 0 0					
Land	7 5 0 0 0	1 2 0 0 0 0				
Total	7 0 0 0 0 0	3 7 5 0 0 0				
Accounts Payable	1 5 4 5 0 0	3 5 0 0 0				
Common Stock:						
Plumb Company	2 0 0 0 0 0					
Strap Company		1 5 0 0 0 0				
Other Contributed Capital:						
Plumb Company	3 0 0 0 0					
Strap Company		3 5 0 0 0				
Retained Earnings from Above	3 1 5 5 0 0	1 5 5 0 0 0				
Minority Interest in Net Assets						
Total	7 0 0 0 0 0	3 7 5 0 0 0				

NAME

SECTION

DATE

PLACER COMPANY AND SUBSIDIARY
Consolidated Statements Workpaper
For the Year Ended December 31, 1992

	Placer Company	Sands Company	Eliminations Debit	Eliminations Credit	Minority Interest	Consolidated Balances
INCOME STATEMENT						
Sales	1 3 4 4 0 0 0	5 0 0 0 0 0				
Equity in Subsidiary Income	9 6 0 5 0					
Interest Income	5 0 0 0					
Total Revenue	1 4 4 5 0 5 0	5 0 0 0 0 0				
Cost of Goods Sold	8 2 2 0 0 0	2 6 3 0 0 0				
Operating Expenses	2 6 8 0 0 0	1 2 4 0 0 0				
Total Cost and Expense	1 0 9 0 0 0 0	3 8 7 0 0 0				
Net/Combined Income	3 5 5 0 5 0	1 1 3 0 0 0				
Minority Interest in Income						
Net Income to Retained Earnings	3 5 5 0 5 0	1 1 3 0 0 0				
RETAINED EARNINGS STATEMENT						
1/1 Retained Earnings:						
Placer Company	7 4 4 4 5 0					
Sands Company		2 1 7 0 0 0				
Net Income from Above	3 5 5 0 5 0	1 1 3 0 0 0				
Dividends Declared:						
Placer Company	(7 0 0 0 0)					
Sands Company		(6 0 0 0 0)				
12/31 Retained Earnings to Balance Sheet	1 0 2 9 5 0 0	2 7 0 0 0 0				

	Placer Company	Sands Company	Eliminations Debit	Eliminations Credit	Minority Interest	Consolidated Balances
BALANCE SHEET						
Cash	120000	78000				
Accounts Receivable	166000	94000				
Notes Receivable	50000					
Inventory	309000	114000				
Investment in Sands Company	527500					
Plant and Equipment	940000	420000				
Land	90000	70000				
Total	2202500	776000				
Accounts Payable	113000	46000				
Notes Payable	300000	100000				
Common Stock:						
Placer Company	500000					
Sands Company		200000				
Other Contributed Capital:						
Placer Company	260000					
Sands Company		160000				
Retained Earnings from Above	1029500	270000				
Minority Interest in Net Assets						
Total	2202500	776000				

NAME _____

SECTION _____

DATE _____

A.

PRICE COMPANY AND SUBSIDIARY
Consolidated Statements Workpaper
For the Year Ended December 31, 1992

	Price Company	Sinc Company	Eliminations Debit	Eliminations Credit	Minority Interest	Consolidated Balances
INCOME STATEMENT						
Sales	210000	80000				
Equity in Subsidiary Income	20800					
Total Revenue	230800	80000				
Cost of Goods Sold	150000	40000				
Operating Expenses	20000	14000				
Total Cost and Expense	170000	54000				
Net/Combined Income	60800	26000				
Minority Interest in Income						
Net Income to Retained Earnings	60800	26000				
RETAINED EARNINGS STATEMENT						
1/1 Retained Earnings:						
Price Company	40000					
Sinc Company		10000				
Net Income from Above	60800	26000				
Dividends Declared:						
Price Company	(20000)					
Sinc Company		(10000)				
12/31 Retained Earnings to						
Balance Sheet	80800	26000				

Copyright © 1991 by John Wiley & Sons, Inc.

NAME

SECTION

DATE

A. (Continued)

BALANCE SHEET	Price Company	Sinc Company	Eliminations Debit	Eliminations Credit	Minority Interest	Consolidated Balances
Cash	22000	13500				
Accounts Receivable	32000	34000				
Inventory	30000	16000				
Investment in Sinc Company	122800					
Plant and Equipment	105000	62000				
Land	29000	34000				
Total	340800	159500				
Accounts Payable	10000	12000				
Other Liabilities	10000	8000				
Common Stock:						
Price Company	180000					
Sinc Company		103500				
Other Contributed Capital:						
Price Company	60000					
Sinc Company		10000				
Retained Earnings from Above	80800	26000				
Minority Interest in Net Assets						
Total	340800	159500				

NAME

SECTION

DATE

B.

PRICE COMPANY AND SUBSIDIARY
Consolidated Statements Workpaper
For the Year Ended December 31, 1993

	Price Company	Sinc Company	Eliminations Debit	Eliminations Credit	Minority Interest	Consolidated Balances
INCOME STATEMENT						
Sales	240000	100000				
Equity in Subsidiary Income	24000					
Total Revenue	264000	100000				
Cost of Goods Sold	170000	52000				
Operating Expenses	30000	18000				
Total Cost and Expense	200000	70000				
Net/Combined Income	64000	30000				
Minority Interest in Income						
Net Income to Retained Earnings	64000	30000				
RETAINED EARNINGS STATEMENT						
1/1 Retained Earnings:						
Price Company	80800					
Sinc Company		26000				
Net Income from Above	64000	30000				
Dividends Declared:						
Price Company	(20000)					
Sinc Company		(15000)				
12/31 Retained Earnings to Balance Sheet	124800	41000				

	Price Company	Sinc Company	Eliminations Debit	Eliminations Credit	Minority Interest	Consolidated Balances
BALANCE SHEET						
Cash	29000	16000				
Accounts Receivable	36000	32000				
Inventory	38000	24000				
Investment in Sinc Company	134800					
Plant and Equipment	124000	70000				
Land	29000	34000				
Total	390800	176000				
Accounts Payable	11000	7000				
Other Liabilities	15000	14500				
Common Stock:						
Price Company	180000					
Sinc Company		103500				
Other Contributed Capital:						
Price Company	60000					
Sinc Company		10000				
Retained Earnings from Above	124800	41000				
Minority Interest in Net Assets						
Total	390800	176000				

NAME

SECTION

DATE

PLOW COMPANY AND SUBSIDIARY
Consolidated Statements Workpaper
For the Year Ended December 31, 1992

	Plow Company	Share Company	Eliminations Debit	Eliminations Credit	Minority Interest	Consolidated Balances
INCOME STATEMENT						
Sales	800000	340000				
Equity in Subsidiary Income	83700					
Interest Income	12500	3000				
Total Revenue	896200	343000				
Cost of Goods Sold	460000	185000				
Operating Expenses	205000	65000				
Total Cost and Expense	665000	250000				
Net/Combined Income	231200	93000				
Minority Interest in Income						
Net Income to Retained Earnings	231200	93000				
RETAINED EARNINGS STATEMENT						
1/1 Retained Earnings:						
Plow Company	548000					
Share Company		290000				
Net Income from Above	231200	93000				
Dividends Declared:						
Plow Company	(50000)					
Share Company		(25000)				
12/31 Retained Earnings to Balance Sheet	729200	358000				

BALANCE SHEET	Plow Company	Share Company	Eliminations Debit	Eliminations Credit	Minority Interest	Consolidated Balances
Cash and Marketable Securities	98000	72000				
Receivables (net)	182000	180000				
Inventory	214000	162000				
Investment in Share Company	509200					
Plant and Equipment	309000	301000				
Land	85000	75000				
Total	1397200	790000				
Accounts Payable	96000	64000				
Accrued Expenses	22000	18000				
Notes Payable	100000	200000				
Common Stock:						
Plow Company	300000					
Share Company		100000				
Other Contributed Capital:						
Plow Company	150000					
Share Company		80000				
Treasury Stock		(30000)				
Retained Earnings from Above	729200	358000				
Minority Interest in Net Assets						
Total	1397200	790000				

NAME

SECTION

DATE

PILLOW COMPANY AND SUBSIDIARY
Consolidated Statements Workpaper
For the Year Ended December 31, 1992

	Pillow Company	Satin Company	Eliminations Debit	Eliminations Credit	Minority Interest	Consolidated Balances
INCOME STATEMENT						
Sales	1 940 000	970 000				
Dividend Income	54 000	6 000				
Total Revenue	1 994 000	976 000				
Cost of Goods Sold	1 261 000	584 000				
Other Expense	484 000	242 000				
Total Cost and Expense	1 745 000	826 000				
Net/Combined Income	249 000	150 000				
Net Income Purchased						
Minority Interest in Income						
Net Income to Retained Earnings	249 000	150 000				
RETAINED EARNINGS STATEMENT						
1/1 Retained Earnings:						
Pillow Company	315 360					
Satin Company		209 200				
Net Income from Above	249 000	150 000				
Dividends Declared:						
Satin Company		(60 000)				
12/31 Retained Earnings to						
Balance Sheet	564 360	299 200				

NAME _____

SECTION _____

DATE _____

BALANCE SHEET	Pillow Company	Satin Company	Eliminations Debit	Eliminations Credit	Minority Interest	Consolidated Balances
Current Assets	390600	179200				
Investment in Satin Company	474000					
Property and Equipment	1334000	562000				
Total	2198600	741200				
Accounts and Notes Payable	270240	124000				
Dividends Payable		60000				
Capital Stock:						
Pillow Company	1000000					
Satin Company		200000				
Other Contributed Capital:						
Pillow Company	364000					
Satin Company		90000				
Treasury Stock		(32000)				
Retained Earnings from Above	564360	299200				
Minority Interest in Net Assets						
Total	2198600	741200				

NAME

SECTION

DATE

PILLOW COMPANY AND SUBSIDIARY
Consolidated Statements Workpaper
For the Year Ended December 31, 1992

	Pillow Company	Satin Company	Eliminations Debit	Eliminations Credit	Minority Interest	Consolidated Balances
INCOME STATEMENT						
Sales	1940000	646666				
Dividend Income	54000	4000				
Total Revenue	1994000	650666				
Cost of Goods Sold	1261000	389334				
Other Expense	484000	161332				
Total Cost and Expense	1745000	550666				
Net/Combined Income	249000	100000				
Minority Interest in Income						
Net Income to Retained Earnings	249000	100000				
RETAINED EARNINGS STATEMENT						
1/1 Retained Earnings - Pillow	315360					
5/1 Retained Earnings - Satin		259200				
Net Income from Above	249000	100000				
Dividends Declared - Satin		(60000)				
12/31 Retained Earnings to Balance Sheet	564360	299200				

NAME

SECTION

DATE

BALANCE SHEET	Pillow Company	Satin Company	Eliminations Debit	Eliminations Credit	Minority Interest	Consolidated Balances
Current Assets	390600	179200				
Investment in Satin Company	474000					
Property and Equipment	1334000	562000				
Total	2198600	741200				
Accounts and Notes Payable	270240	124000				
Dividends Payable		60000				
Capital Stock:						
Pillow Company	1000000					
Satin Company		200000				
Other Contributed Capital:						
Pillow Company	364000					
Satin Company		90000				
Treasury Stock		(32000)				
Retained Earnings from Above	564360	299200				
Minority Interest in Net Assets						
Total	2198600	741200				

NAME

SECTION

DATE

A.

PARK COMPANY AND SUBSIDIARY
Consolidated Statements Workpaper
For the Year Ended December 31, 1992

	Park Company	Salem Company	Eliminations Debit	Eliminations Credit	Minority Interest	Consolidated Balances
INCOME STATEMENT						
Sales	1050000	400000				
Dividend Income	40000					
Total revenue	1090000	400000				
Cost of goods sold	850000	180000				
Depreciation expense	35000	25000				
Other expenses	65000	45000				
Total cost and expense	950000	250000				
Net/combined income	140000	150000				
Minority interest in income						
Net income to retained earnings	140000	150000				
STATEMENT OF RETAINED EARNINGS						
1/1 Retained earnings:						
Park Company	480000					
Salem Company		200000				
Net income from above	140000	150000				
Dividends declared:						
Park Company	(100000)					
Salem Company		(50000)				
12/31 Retained earnings to balance sheet	520000	300000				

NAME _____

SECTION _____

DATE _____

A. (Continued)

BALANCE SHEET	Park Company	Salem Company	Eliminations Debit	Eliminations Credit	Minority Interest	Consolidated Balances
Cash	80000	50000				
Accounts receivable	250000	170000				
Inventory	230000	150000				
Investment in Salem Company	820000					
Difference between cost and						
book value						
Land		300000				
Plant equipment	350000	250000				
Unamortized excess of cost						
over fair value						
Total assets	1730000	920000				
Accounts payable	160000	100000				
Notes payable	50000	200000				
Capital stock						
Park Company	1000000					
Salem Company		500000				
Retained earnings from above	520000	300000				
Minority interest in net assets						
Total liabilities & equity	1730000	920000				

B.

PALMER COMPANY AND SUBSIDIARY
Consolidated Statements Workpaper
For the Year Ended December 31, 1994

	Palmer Company	Salmon Company	Eliminations Debit	Eliminations Credit	Minority Interest	Consolidated Balances
INCOME STATEMENT						
Sales	620000	340000				
Cost of goods sold	430000	240000				
Gross margin	190000	100000				
Depreciation expense	30000	20000				
Amortization of excess of cost						
over fair value						
Other expenses	60000	35000				
Income from operations	100000	45000				
Dividend income	31500					
Net/combined income	131500	45000				
Minority interest in income						
Net income to retained earnings	131500	45000				
STATEMENT OF RETAINED EARNINGS						
1/1 Retained earnings:						
Pamer Company	297600					
Salmon Company		210000				
Net income from above	131500	45000				
Dividends declared:						
Palmer Company	(120000)					
Salmon Company		(35000)				
12/31 Retained earnings to						
balance sheet	309100	220000				

B. (Continued)

BALANCE SHEET	Palmer Company	Salmon Company	Eliminations Debit	Eliminations Credit	Minority Interest	Consolidated Balances
Cash	201200	151000				
Accounts receivable	221000	173000				
Inventory	100400	81000				
Investment in Salmon Company	1000000					
Difference between cost and						
book value						
Equipment	450000	300000				
Accumulated depreciation	(300000)	(140000)				
Land	360000	290000				
Unamortized excess of cost						
over fair value						
Total assets	2032600	855000				
Accounts payable	323500	135000				
Bonds payable	400000					
Capital stock						
Palmer Company	1000000					
Salmon Company		500000				
Retained earnings from above	309100	220000				
Minority interest in net assets						
Total liabilities & equity	2032600	855000				

NAME _____

SECTION _____

DATE _____

B.

PORTER COMPANY AND SUBSIDIARY
Consolidated Statements Workpaper
For the Year Ended December 31, 1992

	Porter Company	Sutton Company	Eliminations Debit	Eliminations Credit	Minority Interest	Consolidated Balances
INCOME STATEMENT						
Sales	105 0000	40 0000				
Equity in Subsidiary Income	12 0000					
Total revenue	117 0000	40 0000				
Cost of goods sold	85 0000	18 0000				
Depreciation expense	3 5000	2 5000				
Other expenses	6 5000	4 5000				
Total cost & expense	95 0000	25 0000				
Net/combined income	22 0000	15 0000				
Minority interest in income						
Net income to retained earnings	22 0000	15 0000				
STATEMENT OF RETAINED EARNINGS						
1/1 Retained earnings						
Porter Company	56 0000					
Sutton Company		20 0000				
Net income from above	22 0000	15 0000				
Dividends declared						
Porter Company	(10 0000)					
Sutton Company		(5 0000)				
12/31 Retained earnings to balance sheet	68 0000	30 0000				

NAME

SECTION

DATE

BALANCE SHEET	Porter Company	Sutton Company	Eliminations Debit	Eliminations Credit	Minority Interest	Consolidated Balances
Cash	80000	50000				
Accounts receivable	250000	170000				
Inventory	230000	150000				
Investment in Sutton Company	980000					
Difference between cost and						
book value						
Land		300000				
Plant and equipment	350000	250000				
Unamortized excess of cost						
over fair value						
Total assets	1890000	920000				
Accounts payable	160000	100000				
Notes payable	50000	20000				
Capital stock						
Porter Company	1000000					
Sutton Company		500000				
Retained earnings from above	680000	300000				
Minority interest in net assets						
Total liabilities & equity	1890000	920000				

NAME _____

SECTION _____

DATE _____

B.

PREISING COMPANY AND SUBSIDIARY
Consolidated Statements Workpaper
For the Year Ended December 31, 1994

	Preising Company	Stevens Company	Eliminations Debit	Eliminations Credit	Minority Interest	Consolidated Balances
INCOME STATEMENT						
Sales	620000	340000				
Cost of goods sold	430000	240000				
Gross margin	190000	100000				
Depreciation expense	30000	20000				
Amortization of excess of cost						
over fair value						
Other expenses	60000	35000				
Income from operations	100000	45000				
Equity in subsidiary income	40500					
Net/combined income	140500	45000				
Minority interest in income						
Net income to retained earnings	140500	45000				
STATEMENT OF RETAINED EARNINGS						
1/1 Retained earnings:						
Preising Company	315600					
Stevens Company		210000				
Net income from above	140500	45000				
Dividends declared:						
Preising Company	(120000)					
Stevens Company		(35000)				
12/31 Retained earnings to						
balance sheet	336100	220000				

B. (Continued)

	Preising Company	Stevens Company	Eliminations Debit	Eliminations Credit	Minority Interest	Consolidated Balances
BALANCE SHEET						
Cash	201200	151000				
Accounts receivable	221000	173000				
Inventory	100400	81000				
Investment in Stevens Company	1027000					
Difference between cost and						
book value						
Equipment	450000	300000				
Accumulated depreciation	(300000)	(140000)				
Land	360000	290000				
Unamortized excess of cost						
over fair value						
Total assets	2059600	855000				
Accounts payable	323500	135000				
Bonds payable	400000					
Capital stock						
Preising Company	1000000					
Stevens Company		500000				
Retained earnings from above	336100	220000				
Minority interest in net assets						
Total liabilities & equity	2059600	855000				

B.

PRESS COMPANY AND SUBSIDIARY
Consolidated Balance Sheet Workpaper
January 1, 1992

	Press Company	Sensor Company	Eliminations Debit	Eliminations Credit	Minority Interest	Consolidated Balances
Cash	265000	38000				
Receivables	422500	76000				
Inventory	216500	124000				
Investment in Sensor Company	800000					
Buildings	465000	322000				
Equipment	229000	246467				
Land	188000	140978				
Patents	167500	190444				
Total	2753500	1137889				
Liabilities	667000	249000				
Common Stock:						
Press Company	700000					
Sensor Company		300000				
Other Contributed Capital:						
Press Company	846000					
Sensor Company		164000				
Retained Earnings:						
Press	540500					
Sensor Company		220000				
Revaluation Capital		204889				
Minority Interest in Net Assets						
Total	2753500	1137889				

NAME

SECTION

DATE

B.

PUSH COMPANY AND SUBSIDIARY
Consolidated Statements Workpaper
For the Year Ended December 31, 1992

	Push Company	Way Down Company	Eliminations Debit	Eliminations Credit	Minority Interest	Consolidated Balances
INCOME STATEMENT						
Sales	1050000	400000				
Dividend Income	40000					
Total revenue	1090000	400000				
Cost of goods sold	850000	180000				
Depreciation expense	35000	50000				
Other expenses	65000	50000				
Total cost and expense	950000	280000				
Net/combined income	140000	120000				
Minority interest in income						
Net income to retained earnings	140000	120000				
STATEMENT OF RETAINED EARNINGS						
1/1 Retained earnings:						
Push Company	480000					
Way Down Company		102500				
Net income from above	140000	120000				
Dividends declared:						
Push Company	(100000)					
Way Down Company		(50000)				
12/31 Retained earnings to balance sheet	520000	172500				

NAME _____

SECTION _____

DATE _____

B. (Continued)

	Push Company	Way Down Company	Eliminations Debit	Eliminations Credit	Minority Interest	Consolidated Balances
BALANCE SHEET						
Cash	80000	50000				
Accounts receivable	250000	170000				
Inventory	230000	150000				
Investment in Way Down Company	820000					
Land	350000	362500				
Plant and equipment		300000				
Goodwill		185000				
Total assets	1730000	1217500				
Accounts payable	160000	100000				
Notes payable	50000	200000				
Revaluation Capital - Way Down Co.		425000				
Capital stock						
Push Company	1000000					
Way Down Company		500000				
Retained earnings from above	520000	172500				
Minority interest in net assets						
Total liabilities & equity	1730000	1217500				

NAME

SECTION

DATE

PARK COMPANY AND SUBSIDIARY
Consolidated Statements Workpaper
For the Year Ended December 31, 1992

	Push Company	Down Company	Eliminations Debit	Eliminations Credit	Minority Interest	Consolidated Balances
INCOME STATEMENT						
Sales	1050000	400000				
Dividend Income	40000					
Total revenue	1090000	400000				
Cost of goods sold	850000	180000				
Depreciation expense	35000	45000				
Other expenses	65000	49000				
Total cost and expense	950000	274000				
Net/combined income	140000	126000				
Minority interest in income						
Net income to retained earnings	140000	126000				
STATEMENT OF RETAINED EARNINGS						
1/1 Retained earnings						
Push Company	480000					
Down Company		122000				
Net income from above	140000	126000				
Dividends declared						
Push Company	(100000)					
Down Company		(50000)				
12/31 Retained earnings to						
balance sheet	520000	198000				

NAME

SECTION

DATE

BALANCE SHEET	Push Company	Down Company	Eliminations Debit	Eliminations Credit	Minority Interest	Consolidated Balances
Cash	80000	50000				
Accounts receivable	250000	170000				
Inventory	230000	150000				
Investment in Down Company	820000					
Land		350000				
Plant and equipment	350000	290000				
Goodwill		148000				
Total assets	1730000	1158000				
Accounts payable	160000	100000				
Notes payable	50000	20000				
Revaluation Capital		340000				
Capital stock						
Push Company	1000000					
Down Company		500000				
Retained earnings from above	520000	198000				
Minority interest in net assets						
Total liabilities & equity	1730000	1158000				

PELL COMPANY AND SUBSIDIARY
Consolidated Statements Workpaper
For the Year Ended December 31, 1992

	Pell Company	Sedbrook Company	Eliminations Debit	Eliminations Credit	Minority Interest	Consolidated Balances
INCOME STATEMENT						
Sales	1100000	530000				
Dividend income	54000					
Total revenue	1154000	530000				
Cost of goods sold:						
Beginning inventory	150000	110000				
Purchases	850000	350000				
Cost of goods available	1000000	460000				
Less ending inventory	140000	115000				
Cost of goods sold	860000	345000				
Other expenses	207000	137500				
Total cost & expense	1067000	482500				
Net/combined income	87000	47500				
Minority interest in income						
Net income to retained earnings	87000	47500				
STATEMENT OF RETAINED EARNINGS						
1/1 Retained earnings						
Pell Company	544000					
Sedbrook Company		120000				
Net income from above	87000	47500				
Dividends declared						
Pell Company	(100000)					
Sedbrook Company		(60000)				
12/31 Retained earnings						
to balance sheet	531000	107500				

NAME

SECTION

DATE

BALANCE SHEET	Pell Company	Sedbrook Company	Eliminations Debit	Eliminations Credit	Minority Interest	Consolidated Balances
Cash	83000	50000				
Accounts receivable	213000	112500				
Inventory	140000	115000				
Investment in Sedbrook Company	540000					
Other assets	500000	400000				
Total assets	1476000	677500				
Accounts payable	70000	30000				
Other liabilities	75000	40000				
Capital stock						
Pell Company	800000					
Sedbrook Company		500000				
Retained earnings from above	531000	107500				
Minority interest in net assets						
Total liabilities & equity	1476000	677500				

NAME _____

SECTION _____

DATE _____

PELL COMPANY AND SUBSIDIARY
Consolidated Statements Workpaper
For the Year Ended December 31, 1992

	Pell Company	Sedbrook Company	Eliminations Debit	Eliminations Credit	Consolidated Income Statement	Consolidated Retained Earnings Statement	Minority Interest	Consolidated Balance Sheet
DEBITS								
Cash	8 3 0 0 0 0	5 0 0 0 0 0						
Accounts Receivable (net)	2 1 3 0 0 0 0	1 1 2 5 0 0 0						
Inventory 1/1	1 5 0 0 0 0 0	1 1 0 0 0 0 0						
Investment in Sedbrook Co.	5 4 0 0 0 0 0							
Other Assets	5 0 0 0 0 0 0	4 0 0 0 0 0 0						
Dividends Declared								
Pell Company	1 0 0 0 0 0 0							
Sedbrook Company		6 0 0 0 0 0						
Purchases	8 5 0 0 0 0 0	3 5 0 0 0 0 0						
Other Expenses	2 0 7 0 0 0 0	1 3 7 5 0 0 0						
Total	2 6 4 3 0 0 0 0	1 2 2 0 0 0 0 0						
Inventory 12/31	1 4 0 0 0 0 0	1 1 1 5 0 0 0						
Total Assets								

NAME _____

SECTION _____

DATE _____

CREDITS	Pell Company	Sedbrook Company	Eliminations Debit	Eliminations Credit	Consolidated Income Statement	Consolidated Retained Earnings Statement	Minority Interest	Consolidated Balance Sheet
Accounts Payable	70000	30000						
Other Liabilities	75000	40000						
Common Stock								
Pell Company	800000							
Sedbrook Company		500000						
Retained Earnings								
Pell Company	544000							
Sedbrook Company		120000						
Sales	1100000	530000						
Dividend Income	54000							
Totals	2643000	1220000						
Inventory 12/31	140000	115000						
Net/Combined Income								
Minority Interest in Income								
Consolidated Net Income								
Consolidated Retained Earnings								
Minority Interest in Net Assets								
Total Liabilities and Equity								

NAME

SECTION

DATE

PENNELL COMPANY AND SUBSIDIARY
Consolidated Statements Workpaper
For the Year Ended December 31, 1992

	Pennell Company	Segal Company	Eliminations Debit	Eliminations Credit	Minority Interest	Consolidated Balances
INCOME STATEMENT						
Sales	1650000	795000				
Dividend income	81000					
Total revenue	1731000	795000				
Cost of goods sold:						
Beginning inventory	225000	165000				
Purchases	1275000	525000				
Less ending inventory	(210000)	(172500)				
Cost of goods sold	1290000	517500				
Other expenses	310500	206250				
Total cost & expense	1600500	723750				
Net/combined income	130500	71250				
Minority interest in income						
Net income to retained earnings	130500	71250				
STATEMENT OF RETAINED EARNINGS						
1/1 Retained earnings						
Pennell Company	811500					
Segal Company		180000				
Net income from above	130500	71250				
Dividends declared						
Pennell Company	(150000)					
Segal Company		(90000)				
12/31 Retained earnings	792000	161250				
to balance sheet						

NAME

SECTION

DATE

BALANCE SHEET	Pennell Company	Segal Company	Eliminations Debit	Eliminations Credit	Minority Interest	Consolidated Balances
Cash	120000	75000				
Accounts receivable	319500	168750				
Inventory	210000	172500				
Investment in Segal Company	810000					
Other assets	750000	600000				
Total assets	2209500	1016250				
Accounts payable	105000	45000				
Other liabilities	112500	60000				
Capital stock						
Pennell Company	1200000					
Segal Company		750000				
Retained earnings from above	792000	161250				
Minority interest in net assets						
Total liabilities & equity	2209500	1016250				

NAME

SECTION

DATE

A.

PENCE COMPANY AND SUBSIDIARY
Consolidated Statements Workpaper
For the Year Ended December 31, 1992

	Pence Company	Selby Company	Eliminations Debit	Eliminations Credit	Minority Interest	Consolidated Balances
INCOME STATEMENT						
Sales	1 3 8 5 0 0 0	7 2 0 0 0 0				
Dividend income	2 4 0 0 0					
Total revenue	1 4 0 9 0 0 0	7 2 0 0 0 0				
Cost of goods sold:						
Beginning inventory	2 1 0 0 0 0	1 5 5 0 0 0				
Purchases	8 7 5 0 0 0	3 6 0 0 0 0				
Cost of goods available	1 0 8 5 0 0 0	5 1 5 0 0 0				
Less ending inventory	4 0 0 0 0 0	2 2 5 0 0 0				
Cost of goods sold	6 8 5 0 0 0	2 9 0 0 0 0				
Other expenses	2 2 5 0 0 0	1 7 0 0 0 0				
Total cost & expense	9 1 0 0 0 0	4 6 0 0 0 0				
Net/combined income	4 9 9 0 0 0	2 6 0 0 0 0				
Minority interest in income						
Net income to retained earnings	4 9 9 0 0 0	2 6 0 0 0 0				
STATEMENT OF RETAINED EARNINGS						
1/1 Retained earnings						
Pence Company	1 4 3 2 7 0 0					
Selby Company		4 5 0 0 0 0				
Net income from above	4 9 9 0 0 0	2 6 0 0 0 0				
Dividends declared						
Pence Company	(4 0 0 0 0)					

NAME

SECTION

DATE

A. (Continued)

	Pence Company	Selby Company	Eliminations Debit	Eliminations Credit	Minority Interest	Consolidated Balances
Selby Company		(30000)				
12/31 Retained earnings						
to balance sheet	1891700	680000				
BALANCE SHEET						
Cash	900000	650000				
Accounts receivable	2970000	850000				
Inventory	4000000	2250000				
Investment in Selby Company	9600000					
Difference between cost & b.v.						
Plant and equipment	8800000	5400000				
Unamortized excess cost over f.v.						
Other assets	3840000	2300000				
Total assets	30111000	11450000				
Accounts payable	2430000	2500000				
Other liabilities	950000	4000000				
Capital stock						
Pence Company	10000000					
Selby Company		4000000				
Retained earnings from above	1891700	680000				
Minority interest in net assets						
Total liabilities & equity	30111000	11450000				

NAME _____

SECTION _____

DATE _____

PRUITT COMPANY AND SUBSIDIARY
Consolidated Statements Workpaper
For the Year Ended December 31, 1992

	Pruitt Company	Stokes Company	Eliminations Debit	Eliminations Credit	Minority Interest	Consolidated Balances
INCOME STATEMENT						
Sales	1 1 0 0 0 0 0	5 3 0 0 0 0				
Equity in subsidiary income	4 2 7 5 0					
Total revenue	1 1 4 2 7 5 0	5 3 0 0 0 0				
Cost of goods sold:						
Beginning inventory	1 5 0 0 0 0	1 1 0 0 0 0				
Purchases	8 5 0 0 0 0	3 5 0 0 0 0				
Cost of goods available	1 0 0 0 0 0 0	4 6 0 0 0 0				
Less ending inventory	1 4 0 0 0 0	1 1 5 0 0 0				
Cost of goods sold	8 6 0 0 0 0	3 4 5 0 0 0				
Other expenses	2 0 7 0 0 0	1 3 7 5 0 0				
Total cost and expense	1 0 6 7 0 0 0	4 8 2 5 0 0				
Net/combined income	7 5 7 5 0	4 7 5 0 0				
Minority interest in income						
Net income to retained earnings	7 5 7 5 0	4 7 5 0 0				
STATEMENT OF RETAINED EARNINGS						
1/1 Retained earnings						
Pruitt Company	5 6 2 0 0 0					
Stokes Company		1 2 0 0 0 0				
Net income from above	7 5 7 5 0	4 7 5 0 0				
Dividends declared						
Pruitt Company	(1 0 0 0 0 0)					
Stokes Company		(6 0 0 0 0)				
12/31 Retained earnings to balance sheet	5 3 7 7 5 0	1 0 7 5 0 0				

NAME
SECTION
DATE

	Pruitt Company	Stokes Company	Eliminations Debit	Eliminations Credit	Minority Interest	Consolidated Balances
BALANCE SHEET						
Cash	83000	50000				
Accounts receivable	213000	112500				
Inventory	140000	115000				
Investment in Stokes Company	546750					
Other assets	500000	400000				
Total assets	1482750	677500				
Accounts payable	70000	30000				
Other liabilities	75000	40000				
Capital stock						
Pruitt Company	800000					
Stokes Company		500000				
Retained earnings from above	537750	107500				
Minority interest in net assets						
Total liabilities & equity	1482750	677500				

PRUITT COMPANY AND SUBSIDIARY
Consolidated Statements Workpaper
For the Year Ended December 31, 1992

	Pruitt Company	Stokes Company	Eliminations Debit	Eliminations Credit	Consolidated Income Statement	Consolidated Retained Earnings Statement	Minority Interest	Consolidated Balance Sheet
DEBITS								
Cash	83000	50000						
Accounts Receivable (net)	213000	112500						
Inventory 1/1	150000	110000						
Investment in Stokes Company	546750							
Other Assets	500000	400000						
Dividends Declared								
Pruitt Company	100000							
Stokes Company		60000						
Purchases	850000	350000						
Other Expenses	207000	137500						
Total	2649750	1220000						
Inventory 12/31	140000	115000						
Total Assets								

Problem 5-12 (Continued)

NAME

SECTION

DATE

CREDITS	Pruitt Company	Stokes Company	Eliminations Debit	Eliminations Credit	Consolidated Income Statement	Consolidated Retained Earnings Statement	Minority Interest	Consolidated Balance Sheet
Accounts Payable	70000	30000						
Other Liabilities	75000	40000						
Common Stock								
Pruitt Company	800000							
Stokes Company		500000						
Retained Earnings								
Pruitt Company	562000							
Stokes Company		120000						
Sales	1100000	530000						
Equity in Subsidiary Income	42750							
Totals	2649750	1220000						
Inventory 12/31	140000	115000						
Net/Combined Income								
Minority Interest in Income								
Consolidated Net Income								
Consolidated Retained Earnings								
Minority Interest in Net Assets								
Total Liabilities and Equity								

Copyright © 1991 by John Wiley & Sons, Inc.

PAQUE COMPANY AND SUBSIDIARY
Consolidated Statements Workpaper
For the Year Ended December 31, 1992

	Paque Company	Slade Company	Eliminations Debit	Eliminations Credit	Minority Interest	Consolidated Balances
INCOME STATEMENT						
Sales	1 6 5 0 0 0 0	7 9 5 0 0 0				
Equity in subsidiary income	6 4 1 2 5					
Total revenue	1 7 1 4 1 2 5	7 9 5 0 0 0				
Cost of goods sold:						
Beginning inventory	2 2 5 0 0 0	1 6 5 0 0 0				
Purchases	1 2 7 5 0 0 0	5 2 5 0 0 0				
Less ending inventory	(2 1 0 0 0 0)	(1 7 2 5 0 0)				
Cost of goods sold	1 2 9 0 0 0 0	5 1 7 5 0 0				
Other expenses	3 1 0 5 0 0	2 0 6 2 5 0				
Total cost and expense	1 6 0 0 5 0 0	7 2 3 7 5 0				
Net/combined income	1 1 3 6 2 5	7 1 2 5 0				
Minority interest in income						
Net income to retained earnings	1 1 3 6 2 5	7 1 2 5 0				
STATEMENT OF RETAINED EARNINGS						
1/1 Retained earnings						
Paque Company	8 3 8 5 0 0					
Slade Company		1 8 0 0 0 0				
Net income from above	1 1 3 6 2 5	7 1 2 5 0				
Dividends declared						
Paque Company	(1 5 0 0 0 0)					
Slade Company		(9 0 0 0 0)				
12/31 Retained earnings to balance sheet	8 0 2 1 2 5	1 6 1 2 5 0				

BALANCE SHEET	Paque Company	Slade Company	Eliminations Debit	Eliminations Credit	Minority Interest	Consolidated Balances
Cash	120000	75000				
Accounts receivable	319500	168750				
Inventory	210000	172500				
Investment in Slade Company	820125					
Other assets	750000	600000				
Total assets	2219625	1016250				
Accounts payable	105000	45000				
Other liabilities	112500	60000				
Capital stock						
Paque Company	1200000					
Slade Company		750000				
Retained earnings from above	802125	161250				
Minority interest in net assets						
Total liabilities & equity	2219625	1016250				

NAME

SECTION

DATE

PERRY COMPANY AND SUBSIDIARY
Consolidated Statements Workpaper
For the Year Ended December 31, 1992

	Perry Company	Sloane Company	Eliminations Debit	Eliminations Credit	Minority Interest	Consolidated Balances
INCOME STATEMENT						
Sales	1 3 8 5 0 0 0	7 2 0 0 0 0				
Equity in subsidiary income	2 0 8 0 0 0					
Total revenue	1 5 9 3 0 0 0	7 2 0 0 0 0				
Cost of goods sold:						
Beginning inventory	2 1 0 0 0 0	1 5 5 0 0 0				
Purchases	8 7 5 0 0 0	3 6 0 0 0 0				
Cost of goods available	1 0 8 5 0 0 0	5 1 5 0 0 0				
Less ending inventory	4 0 0 0 0 0	2 2 5 0 0 0				
Cost of goods sold	6 8 5 0 0 0	2 9 0 0 0 0				
Other expenses	2 2 5 0 0 0	1 7 0 0 0 0				
Total cost and expense	9 1 0 0 0 0	4 6 0 0 0 0				
Net/combined income	6 8 3 0 0 0	2 6 0 0 0 0				
Minority interest in income						
Net income to retained earnings	6 8 3 0 0 0	2 6 0 0 0 0				
STATEMENT OF RETAINED EARNINGS						
1/1 Retained earnings						
Perry Company	1 4 7 2 7 0 0					
Sloane Company		4 5 0 0 0 0				
Net income from above	6 8 3 0 0 0	2 6 0 0 0 0				
Dividends declared						
Perry Company	(4 0 0 0 0 0)					

NAME

SECTION

DATE

	Perry Company	Sloane Company	Eliminations Debit	Eliminations Credit	Minority Interest	Consolidated Balances
Sloane Company		(3 0 0 0 0)				
12/31 Retained earnings to balance sheet	2 1 1 5 7 0 0	6 8 0 0 0 0				
BALANCE SHEET						
Cash	9 0 0 0 0	6 5 0 0 0				
Accounts receivable	2 9 7 0 0 0	8 5 0 0 0				
Inventory	4 0 0 0 0 0	2 2 5 0 0 0				
Investment in Sloane Company	1 1 8 4 0 0 0					
Difference between cost & book value						
Plant and equipment	8 8 0 0 0 0	5 4 0 0 0 0				
Unamortized excess cost over f.v.						
Other assets	3 8 4 0 0 0	2 3 0 0 0 0				
Total assets	3 2 3 5 0 0 0	1 1 4 5 0 0 0				
Accounts payable	2 4 3 0 0 0	2 5 0 0 0				
Other liabilities	9 5 0 0 0	4 0 0 0 0				
Capital stock						
Perry Company	1 0 0 0 0 0 0					
Sloane Company		4 0 0 0 0 0				
Retained earnings from above	2 1 1 5 7 0 0	6 8 0 0 0 0				
Minority interest in net assets						
Total liabilities & equity	3 2 3 5 0 0 0	1 1 4 5 0 0 0				

NAME

SECTION

DATE

A.

PIERCE COMPANY AND SUBSIDIARY
Consolidated Statements Workpaper
For the Year Ended December 31, 1992

	Pierce Company	Sexton Company	Eliminations Debit	Eliminations Credit	Minority Interest	Consolidated Balances
INCOME STATEMENT						
Sales	1 4 7 5 0 0 0	1 1 1 0 0 0 0				
Dividend Income	8 0 0 0 0					
Total revenue	1 5 5 5 0 0 0	1 1 1 0 0 0 0				
Cost of goods sold	9 4 2 0 0 0	7 9 5 0 0 0				
Income tax expense	1 8 7 2 0 0	9 0 0 0 0				
Other expenses	1 4 5 0 0 0	9 0 0 0 0				
Total cost & expense	1 2 7 4 2 0 0	9 7 5 0 0 0				
Net/combined income	2 8 0 8 0 0	1 3 5 0 0 0				
Minority interest in income						
Net income to retained earnings	2 8 0 8 0 0	1 3 5 0 0 0				
STATEMENT OF RETAINED EARNINGS						
1/1 Retained earnings						
Pierce Company	1 3 0 0 0 0 0					
Sexton Company		1 0 4 0 0 0 0				
Net income from above	2 8 0 8 0 0	1 3 5 0 0 0				
Dividends declared						
Pierce Company	(1 2 0 0 0 0)					
Sexton Company		(1 0 0 0 0 0)				
12/31 Retained earnings						
to balance sheet	1 4 6 0 8 0 0	1 0 7 5 0 0 0				

A. (Continued)

BALANCE SHEET	Pierce Company	Sexton Company	Eliminations Debit	Eliminations Credit	Minority Interest	Consolidated Balances
Current assets	5 6 8 0 0 0	2 7 1 0 0 0				
Investment in Sexton Company	1 6 0 0 0 0 0					
Plant and equipment	1 9 7 2 0 0 0	8 3 0 0 0 0				
Accumulated depreciation	(3 7 5 0 0 0)	(2 9 0 0 0 0)				
Other assets	1 0 0 0 8 0 0	1 6 0 0 0 0 0				
Total assets	4 7 6 5 8 0 0	2 4 1 1 0 0 0				
Other liabilities	3 0 5 0 0 0	1 3 6 0 0 0				
Capital stock						
Pierce Company	3 0 0 0 0 0 0					
Sexton Company		1 2 0 0 0 0 0				
Retained earnings from above	1 4 6 0 8 0 0	1 0 7 5 0 0 0				
Minority interest in net assets						
Total liabilities & equity	4 7 6 5 8 0 0	2 4 1 1 0 0 0				

NAME _____

SECTION _____

DATE _____

PIERCE COMPANY AND SUBSIDIARY
Consolidated Statements Workpaper
For the Year Ended December 31, 1992

DEBITS	Pierce Company	Sexton Company	Eliminations Debit	Eliminations Credit	Consolidated Income Statement	Consolidated Retained Earnings Statement	Minority Interest	Consolidated Balance Sheet
Current Assets	568000	271000						
Investment in Sexton Company	1600000							
Fixed Assets	1972000	830000						
Other Assets	1000800	160000						
Dividends Declared								
Pierce Company	120000							
Sexton Company		100000						
Cost of Goods Sold	942000	795000						
Other Expenses	145000	90000						
Income Tax Expense	187200	90000						
Totals	6535000	3776000						

Copyright © 1991 by John Wiley & Sons, Inc.

NAME

SECTION

DATE

	Pierce Company	Sexton Company	Eliminations Debit	Eliminations Credit	Consolidated Income Statement	Consolidated Retained Earnings Statement	Minority Interest	Consolidated Balance Sheet
CREDITS								
Liabilities	305000	136000						
Accumulated Depreciation	375000	290000						
Common Stock								
Pierce Company	3000000							
Sexton Company		1200000						
Retained Earnings								
Pierce Company	1300000							
Sexton Company		1040000						
Sales	1475000	1110000						
Dividend Income	80000							
Totals	6535000	3776000						
Net/Combined Income								
Minority Interest in Income								
Consolidated Net Income								
Consolidated Retained Earnings								
Minority Interest in Net Assets								
Total Liabilities and Equity								

PITTS COMPANY AND SUBSIDIARY
Consolidated Statements Workpaper
For the Year Ended December 31, 1993

	Pitts Company	Shannon Company	Eliminations Debit	Eliminations Credit	Minority Interest	Consolidated Balances
INCOME STATEMENT						
Sales	1 9 5 0 0 0 0	1 3 5 0 0 0 0				
Dividend income	6 0 0 0 0					
Total revenue	2 0 1 0 0 0 0	1 3 5 0 0 0 0				
Cost of goods sold	1 3 5 0 0 0 0	9 0 0 0 0 0				
Other expenses	2 2 5 0 0 0	1 5 0 0 0 0				
Total cost & expense	1 5 7 5 0 0 0	1 0 5 0 0 0 0				
Net/combined income	4 3 5 0 0 0	3 0 0 0 0 0				
Minority interest in income						
Net income to retained earnings	4 3 5 0 0 0	3 0 0 0 0 0				
STATEMENT OF RETAINED EARNINGS						
1/1 Retained earnings						
Pitts Company	1 2 1 5 0 0 0					
Shannon Company		1 0 3 8 0 0 0				
Net income from above	4 3 5 0 0 0	3 0 0 0 0 0				
Dividends declared						
Pitts Company	(1 5 0 0 0 0)					
Shannon Company		(7 5 0 0 0)				
12/31 Retained earnings	1 5 0 0 0 0 0	1 2 6 3 0 0 0				
to balance sheet						

NAME

SECTION

DATE

BALANCE SHEET	Pitts Company	Shannon Company	Eliminations Debit	Eliminations Credit	Minority Interest	Consolidated Balances
Inventory	498000	225000				
Investment in Shannon Company	960000					
Plant and equipment	2168100	2625000				
Accumulated depreciation	(900000)	(612000)				
Total assets	2726100	2238000				
Liabilities	465600	450000				
Capital stock						
Pitts Company	760500					
Shannon Company		525000				
Retained earnings from above	1500000	1263000				
Minority interest in net assets						
Total liabilities & equity	2726100	2238000				

NAME

SECTION

DATE

PINKARD COMPANY AND SUBSIDIARY
Consolidated Statements Workpaper
For the Year Ended December 31, 1994

	Pinkard Company	Sheppard Company	Eliminations Debit	Eliminations Credit	Minority Interest	Consolidated Balances
INCOME STATEMENT						
Sales	2 5 5 5 5 0 0	1 1 2 0 0 0 0				
Dividend income	5 4 0 0 0					
Total revenue	2 6 0 9 5 0 0	1 1 2 0 0 0 0				
Cost of goods sold	1 7 3 0 0 0 0	6 9 0 5 0 0				
Expenses	6 5 4 5 0 0	2 5 1 0 0 0				
Total cost & expense	2 3 8 4 5 0 0	9 4 1 5 0 0				
Net/combined income	2 2 5 0 0 0	1 7 8 5 0 0				
Minority interest in income						
Net income to retained earnings	2 2 5 0 0 0	1 7 8 5 0 0				
STATEMENT OF RETAINED EARNINGS						
1/1 Retained earnings						
Pinkard Company	5 9 5 0 0 0					
Sheppard Company		1 3 9 5 0 0				
Net income from above	2 2 5 0 0 0	1 7 8 5 0 0				
Dividends declared						
Pinkard Company	(1 0 0 0 0 0)					
Sheppard Company		(6 0 0 0 0)				
12/31 Retained earnings to balance sheet	7 2 0 0 0 0	2 5 8 0 0 0				

BALANCE SHEET	Pinkard Company	Sheppard Company	Eliminations Debit	Eliminations Credit	Minority Interest	Consolidated Balances
Cash	119500	132500				
Accounts receivable	342000	125000				
Inventory	362000	201000				
Other current assets	40500	13000				
Investment in Sheppard Company	426000					
Difference between cost and book value						
Land	150000					
Plant and equipment	825000	241000				
Accumulated depreciation	(207000)	(53500)				
Manufacturing formula						
Total assets	2058000	659000				
Accounts payable	295000	32000				
Other liabilities	43000	19000				
Capital stock						
Pinkard Company	1000000					
Sheppard Company		300000				
Additional paid-in capital						
Sheppard Company		50000				
Retained earnings from above	720000	258000				
Minority interest in net assets						
Total liabilities & equity	2058000	659000				

NAME

SECTION

DATE

PLUM COMPANY AND SUBSIDIARY
Consolidated Statements Workpaper
For the Year Ended December 31, 1992

	Plum Company	Sower Company	Eliminations Debit	Eliminations Credit	Minority Interest	Consolidated Balances
INCOME STATEMENT						
Sales	1 2 9 1 5 0 0	5 6 0 0 0 0				
Other income		1 4 0 0 0 0				
Dividend income	4 2 5 0 0					
Total revenue	1 3 3 4 0 0 0	7 0 0 0 0 0				
Cost of goods sold	6 6 0 0 0 0	3 0 0 0 0 0				
Depreciation expense	1 3 8 0 0 0	2 0 0 0 0				
Interest expense	8 0 0 0	1 0 0 0 0				
Other expenses	1 7 4 0 0 0	1 4 0 0 0 0				
Total cost and expense	9 8 0 0 0 0	4 7 0 0 0 0				
Net/combined income	3 5 4 0 0 0	2 3 0 0 0 0				
Minority interest in income						
Net income to retained earnings	3 5 4 0 0 0	2 3 0 0 0 0				
STATEMENT OF RETAINED EARNINGS						
1/1 Retained earnings						
Plum Company	3 5 0 5 0 0					
Sower Company		2 5 0 0 0 0				
Net income from above	3 5 4 0 0 0	2 3 0 0 0 0				
Dividends declared						
Plum Company	(1 0 0 0 0 0)					
Sower Company		(5 0 0 0 0)				
12/31 Retained earnings to bal. sheet	6 0 4 5 0 0	4 3 0 0 0 0				

NAME

SECTION

DATE

BALANCE SHEET	Plum Company	Sower Company	Eliminations Debit	Eliminations Credit	Minority Interest	Consolidated Balances
Cash	127000	70000				
Accounts receivable	300000	210000				
Inventory	270000	175000				
Investment in Sower Company	955000					
Difference between cost and book value						
Land	100000	390000				
Plant and equipment	800000	700000				
Accumulated depreciation	(200000)	(200000)				
Unamortized discount on bonds payable						
Unamortized excess of cost over fair value						
Total assets	2352000	1345000				
Accounts payable	167500	65000				
Bonds payable	80000	100000				
Capital stock						
Plum Company	1500000					
Sower Company		750000				
Retained earnings from above	604500	430000				
Minority interest in net assets						
Total liabilities & equity	2352000	1345000				

NAME

SECTION

DATE

PITMAN COMPANY AND SUBSIDIARY
Consolidated Statements Workpaper
For the Year Ended December 31, 1993

	Pitman Company	Shelton Company	Eliminations Debit	Eliminations Credit	Minority Interest	Consolidated Balances
INCOME STATEMENT						
Sales	1 7 0 0 0 0 0	9 0 0 0 0 0				
Gain on sale of land		5 0 0 0 0				
Dividend income	6 3 0 0 0					
Total revenue	1 7 6 3 0 0 0	9 5 0 0 0 0				
Cost of goods sold	6 0 0 0 0 0	4 0 0 0 0 0				
Depreciation expense	6 0 0 0 0 0	4 0 0 0 0				
Other expenses	4 0 0 0 0 0	2 6 0 0 0 0				
Total cost & expense	1 0 6 0 0 0 0	7 0 0 0 0 0				
Net/combined income	7 0 3 0 0 0	2 5 0 0 0 0				
Minority interest in income						
Net income to retained earnings	7 0 3 0 0 0	2 5 0 0 0 0				
STATEMENT OF RETAINED EARNINGS						
1/1 Retained earnings						
Pitman Company	7 0 6 0 0 0					
Shelton Company		5 8 0 0 0 0				
Net income from above	7 0 3 0 0 0	2 5 0 0 0 0				
Dividends declared						
Pitman Company	(1 2 0 0 0 0)					
Shelton Company		(7 0 0 0 0)				
12/31 Retained earnings to balance sheet	1 2 8 9 0 0 0	7 6 0 0 0 0				

BALANCE SHEET	Pitman Company	Shelton Company	Eliminations Debit	Eliminations Credit	Minority Interest	Consolidated Balances
Cash	200000	150000				
Accounts receivable	300000	250000				
Inventory	300000	250000				
Marketable securities	100000	200000				
Investment in Shelton Company	1480000					
Difference between cost and book value						
Land	400000	350000				
Plant and equipment	1000000	800000				
Total assets	3780000	2000000				
Accounts payable	241000	140000				
Notes payable	350000	100000				
Capital stock						
Pitman Company	1900000					
Shelton Company		1000000				
Retained earnings from above	1289000	760000				
Minority interest in net assets						
Total liabilities & equity	3780000	2000000				

NAME

SECTION

DATE

PROUT COMPANY AND SUBSIDIARY
Consolidated Statements Workpaper
For the Year Ended December 31, 1992

	Prout Company	Stahl Company	Eliminations Debit	Eliminations Credit	Minority Interest	Consolidated Balances
INCOME STATEMENT						
Sales	1 4 7 5 0 0 0	1 1 1 0 0 0 0				
Equity in Subsidiary Income	1 0 8 0 0 0					
Total revenue	1 5 8 3 0 0 0	1 1 1 0 0 0 0				
Cost of goods sold	9 4 2 0 0 0	7 9 5 0 0 0				
Income tax expense	1 8 7 2 0 0	9 0 0 0 0				
Other expenses	1 4 5 0 0 0	9 0 0 0 0				
Total cost & expense	1 2 7 4 2 0 0	9 7 5 0 0 0				
Net/combined income	3 0 8 8 0 0	1 3 5 0 0 0				
Minority interest in income						
Net income to retained earnings	3 0 8 8 0 0	1 3 5 0 0 0				
STATEMENT OF RETAINED EARNINGS						
1/1 Retained earnings						
Prout Company	1 4 9 2 0 0 0					
Stahl Company		1 0 4 0 0 0 0				
Net income from above	3 0 8 8 0 0	1 3 5 0 0 0				
Dividends declared						
Prout Company	(1 2 0 0 0 0)					
Stahl Company		(1 0 0 0 0 0)				
12/31 Retained earnings						
to balance sheet	1 6 8 0 8 0 0	1 0 7 5 0 0 0				

NAME

SECTION

DATE

BALANCE SHEET	Prout Company	Stahl Company	Eliminations Debit	Eliminations Credit	Minority Interest	Consolidated Balances
Current assets	568000	271000				
Investment in Stahl Company	1820000					
Plant and equipment	1972000	830000				
Accumulated depreciation	(375000)	(290000)				
Other assets	1000800	1600000				
Total assets	4985800	2411000				
Other liabilities	305000	136000				
Capital stock						
Prout Company	3000000					
Stahl Company		1200000				
Retained earnings from above	1680800	1075000				
Minority interest in net assets						
Total liabilities & equity	4985800	2411000				

NAME

SECTION

DATE

PROUT COMPANY AND SUBSIDIARY
Consolidated Statements Workpaper
For the Year Ended December 31, 1992

	Prout Company	Stahl Company	Eliminations Debit	Eliminations Credit	Consolidated Income Statement	Consolidated Retained Earnings Statement	Minority Interest	Consolidated Balance Sheet
DEBITS								
Current Assets	5680000	2710000						
Investment in Stahl Company	1820000							
Fixed Assets	1972000	830000						
Other Assets	1000800	1600000						
Dividends Declared								
Prout Company	1200000							
Stahl Company		1000000						
Cost of Goods Sold	942000	795000						
Other Expenses	145000	90000						
Income Tax Expense	187200	90000						
Totals	6755000	3776000						

NAME

SECTION

DATE

CREDITS	Prout Company	Stahl Company	Eliminations Debit	Eliminations Credit	Consolidated Income Statement	Consolidated Retained Earnings Statement	Minority Interest	Consolidated Balance Sheet
Liabilities	305000	136000						
Accumulated Depreciation	375000	290000						
Common Stock								
Prout Company	3000000							
Stahl Company		1200000						
Retained Earnings								
Prout Company	1492000							
Stahl Company		1040000						
Sales	1475000	1110000						
Equity in Subsidiary Income	108000							
Totals	6755000	3776000						
Net/Combined Income								
Minority Interest in Income								
Consolidated Net Income								
Consolidated Retained Earnings								
Minority Interest in Net Assets								
Total Liabilities and Equity								

NAME

SECTION

DATE

PARCH COMPANY AND SUBSIDIARY
Consolidated Statements Workpaper
For the Year Ended December 31, 1993

	Parch Company	Stabler Company	Eliminations Debit	Eliminations Credit	Minority Interest	Consolidated Balances
INCOME STATEMENT						
Sales	1 9 5 0 0 0 0	1 3 5 0 0 0 0				
Equity in Subsidiary Income	2 4 0 0 0 0					
Total revenue	2 1 9 0 0 0 0	1 3 5 0 0 0 0				
Cost of goods sold	1 3 5 0 0 0 0	9 0 0 0 0 0				
Other expenses	2 2 5 0 0 0	1 5 0 0 0 0				
Total cost and expense	1 5 7 5 0 0 0	1 0 5 0 0 0 0				
Net/combined income	6 1 5 0 0 0	3 0 0 0 0 0				
Minority interest in income						
Net income to retained earnings	6 1 5 0 0 0	3 0 0 0 0 0				
STATEMENT OF RETAINED EARNINGS						
1/1 Retained earnings						
Parch Company	1 5 0 5 4 0 0					
Stabler Company		1 0 3 8 0 0 0				
Net income from above	6 1 5 0 0 0	3 0 0 0 0 0				
Dividends declared						
Parch Company	(1 5 0 0 0 0)					
Stabler Company		(7 5 0 0 0)				
12/31 Retained earnings	1 9 7 0 4 0 0	1 2 6 3 0 0 0				
to balance sheet						

NAME

SECTION

DATE

	Parch Company	Stabler Company	Eliminations Debit	Eliminations Credit	Minority Interest	Consolidated Balances
BALANCE SHEET						
Inventory	498000	225000				
Investment in Stabler Company	1430400					
Plant and equipment	2168100	2625000				
Accumulated depreciation	(900000)	(612000)				
Total assets	3196500	2238000				
Liabilities	465600	450000				
Capital stock						
Parch Company	760500					
Stabler Company		525000				
Retained earnings from above	1970400	1263000				
Minority interest in net assets						
Total liabilities & equity	3196500	2238000				

NAME

SECTION

DATE

PARELLA COMPANY AND SUBSIDIARY
Consolidated Statements Workpaper
For the Year Ended December 31, 1994

	Parella Company	Snep Company	Eliminations Debit	Eliminations Credit	Minority Interest	Consolidated Balances
INCOME STATEMENT						
Sales	2 5 5 5 5 0 0	1 1 2 0 0 0 0				
Equity in Subsidiary Income	1 6 0 6 5 0					
Total revenue	2 7 1 6 1 5 0	1 1 2 0 0 0 0				
Cost of goods sold	1 7 3 0 0 0 0	6 9 0 5 0 0				
Expenses	6 5 4 5 0 0	2 5 1 0 0 0				
Total cost & expense	2 3 8 4 5 0 0	9 4 1 5 0 0				
Net/combined income	3 3 1 6 5 0	1 7 8 5 0 0				
Minority interest in income						
Net income to retained earnings	3 3 1 6 5 0	1 7 8 5 0 0				
STATEMENT OF RETAINED EARNINGS						
1/1 Retained earnings						
Parella Company	6 6 6 5 5 0					
Snep Company		1 3 9 5 0 0				
Net income from above	3 3 1 6 5 0	1 7 8 5 0 0				
Dividends declared						
Parella Company	(1 0 0 0 0 0)					
Snep Company		(6 0 0 0 0)				
12/31 Retained earnings to bal. sheet	8 9 8 2 0 0	2 5 8 0 0 0				

NAME

SECTION

DATE

BALANCE SHEET	Parella Company	Snep Company	Eliminations Debit	Eliminations Credit	Minority Interest	Consolidated Balances
Cash	119500	132500				
Accounts receivable	342000	125000				
Inventory	362000	201000				
Other current assets	40500	13000				
Investment in Snep Company	604200					
Difference between cost and book value						
Land	150000					
Plant and equipment	825000	241000				
Accumulated depreciation	(207000)	(53500)				
Manufacturing formula						
Total assets	2236200	659000				
Accounts payable	295000	32000				
Other liabilities	43000	19000				
Capital stock						
Parella Company	1000000					
Snep Company		300000				
Additional paid-in capital						
Snep Company		50000				
Retained earnings from above	898200	258000				
Minority interest in net assets						
Total liabilities & equity	2236200	659000				

NAME

SECTION

DATE

PEAT COMPANY AND SUBSIDIARY
Consolidated Statements Workpaper
March 1, 1992

	Peat Company	Snap Company	Eliminations Debit	Eliminations Credit	Consolidated Balances
Cash	600000	165000			
Receivables	90000	97500			
Inventories	480000	285000			
Investment in Snap Company	554400				
Property, Plant & Equipment	675000	300000			
Patents	52500				
Total	2451900	847500			
Current liabilities	78000	66500			
Long-term liabilities	412500	165000			
Common Stock:					
Peat Company	1500000				
Snap Company		450000			
Other Contributed Capital:					
Peat Company	151500				
Snap Company		135000			
Retained Earnings:					
Peat Company	309900				
Snap Company		31000			
Total	2451900	847500			

NAME

SECTION

DATE

PAN COMPANY AND SUBSIDIARY
Consolidated Balance Sheet Workpaper
January 1, 1992

	Pan Company	Smile Company	Eliminations Debit	Eliminations Credit	Consolidated Balances
Cash	3 0 0 0 0 0	2 8 0 0 0 0			
Other Current Assets	1 3 3 0 0 0 0	3 9 0 0 0 0			
Investment in Smile Company	9 5 0 0 0 0	- 0 -			
Long-Term Assets	3 0 0 0 0 0 0	5 2 0 0 0 0			
Other Assets	5 0 0 0 0				
Total	5 6 3 0 0 0 0	1 1 9 0 0 0 0			
Current Liabilities	9 7 0 0 0 0	1 9 0 0 0 0			
Bonds Payable	4 0 0 0 0 0				
Common Stock:					
Pan Company	3 1 2 0 0 0 0				
Smile Company		5 0 0 0 0 0			
Treasury stock at par		(5 0 0 0 0)			
Other Contributed Capital:					
Pan Company	7 4 5 0 0 0				
Smile Company		2 5 0 0 0 0			
Retained Earnings:					
Pan Company	3 9 5 0 0 0				
Smile Company		3 0 0 0 0 0			
Total	5 6 3 0 0 0 0	1 1 9 0 0 0 0			

NAME

SECTION

DATE

PLANE COMPANY AND SUBSIDIARY
Consolidated Statement Workpaper
For the Year Ended December 31, 1992

	Plane Company	Star Company	Eliminations Debit	Eliminations Credit	Minority Interest	Consolidated Balances
INCOME STATEMENT						
Sales	680000	420000				
Dividend Income	28500					
Total Revenue	708500	420000				
Cost of Goods Sold	442000	234000				
Other Expense	110000	96000				
Total Cost and Expense	552000	330000				
Net/Combined Income	156500	90000				
Minority Interest in Income						
Net Income to Retained Earnings	156500	90000				
RETAINED EARNINGS STATEMENT						
1/1 Retained Earnings:						
Plane Company	348000					
Star Company		154000				
Net Income from Above	156500	90000				
Dividends Declared:						
Plane Company	(50000)					
Star Company		(30000)				
12/31 Retained Earnings to Balance Sheet	454500	214000				

NAME _____

SECTION _____

DATE _____

BALANCE SHEET	Plane Company	Star Company	Eliminations Debit	Eliminations Credit	Minority Interest	Consolidated Balances
Current Assets	3 2 1 2 0 0	1 6 4 0 0 0				
Investment in Star Company	2 2 2 3 0 0					
Plant Assets	6 6 5 0 0 0	3 4 2 0 0 0				
Total	1 2 0 8 5 0 0	5 0 6 0 0 0				
Liabilities	1 5 4 0 0 0	9 2 0 0 0				
Common Stock:						
Plane Company	6 0 0 0 0 0					
Star Company		2 0 0 0 0 0				
Retained Earnings from Above	4 5 4 5 0 0	2 1 4 0 0 0				
Minority Interest in Net Assets						
Total	1 2 0 8 5 0 0	5 0 6 0 0 0				

NAME

SECTION

DATE

PLANE COMPANY AND SUBSIDIARY
Consolidated Statements Workpaper
For the Year Ended December 31, 1992

	Plane Company	Star Company	Eliminations Debit	Eliminations Credit	Minority Interest	Consolidated Balances
INCOME STATEMENT						
Sales	6 8 0 0 0 0	4 2 0 0 0 0				
Equity in Subsidiary Income	8 5 5 0 0					
Total Revenue	7 6 5 5 0 0	4 2 0 0 0 0				
Cost of Goods Sold	4 4 2 0 0 0	2 3 4 0 0 0				
Other Expense	1 1 0 0 0 0	9 6 0 0 0				
Total Cost and Expense	5 5 2 0 0 0	3 3 0 0 0 0				
Net/Combined Income	2 1 3 5 0 0	9 0 0 0 0				
Minority Interest in Income						
Net Income to Retained Earnings	2 1 3 5 0 0	9 0 0 0 0				
RETAINED EARNINGS STATEMENT						
1/1 Retained Earnings:						
Plane Company	4 6 2 0 0 0					
Star Company		1 5 4 0 0 0				
Net Income from Above	2 1 3 5 0 0	9 0 0 0 0				
Dividends Declared:						
Plane Company	(5 0 0 0 0)					
Star Company		(3 0 0 0 0)				
12/31 Retained Earnings to Balance Sheet	6 2 5 5 0 0	2 1 4 0 0 0				

NAME

SECTION

DATE

	Plane Company	Star Company	Eliminations Debit	Eliminations Credit	Minority Interest	Consolidated Balances
BALANCE SHEET						
Current Assets	3 2 1 2 0 0	1 6 4 0 0 0				
Investment in Star Company	3 9 3 3 0 0					
Plant Assets	6 6 5 0 0 0	3 4 2 0 0 0				
Total	1 3 7 9 5 0 0	5 0 6 0 0 0				
Liabilities	1 5 4 0 0 0	9 2 0 0 0				
Common Stock:						
Plane Company	6 0 0 0 0 0					
Star Company		2 0 0 0 0 0				
Retained Earnings from Above	6 2 5 5 0 0	2 1 4 0 0 0				
Minority Interest in Net Assets						
Total	1 3 7 9 5 0 0	5 0 6 0 0 0				

NAME

SECTION

DATE

PENTA COMPANY AND SUBSIDIARY
Consolidated Statements Workpaper
For the Year Ended December 31, 1992

	Penta Company	Sells Company	Eliminations Debit	Eliminations Credit	Minority Interest	Consolidated Balances
INCOME STATEMENT						
Sales	1100000	530000				
Dividend Income	21000					
Total Revenue	1121000	530000				
Cost of Goods Sold:						
Beginning Inventory	150000	110000				
Purchases	850000	350000				
Cost of Goods Available	1000000	460000				
Less Ending Inventory	140000	115000				
Cost of Goods Sold	860000	345000				
Income Tax Expense	32000	20500				
Other Expenses	175000	117000				
Total Cost and Expense	1067000	482500				
Net/Combined Income	54000	47500				
Minority Interest in Income						
Net Income to Retained Earnings	54000	47500				
STATEMENT OF RETAINED EARNINGS						
1/1 Retained Earnings						
Penta Company	541000					
Sells Company		320000				

NAME

SECTION

DATE

	Penta Company	Sells Company	Eliminations Debit	Eliminations Credit	Minority Interest	Consolidated Balances
Net Income from Above	5 4 0 0 0	4 7 5 0 0				
Dividends Declared						
Penta Company	(1 0 0 0 0 0)					
Sells Company		(3 0 0 0 0)				
12/31 Retained Earnings to						
Balance Sheet	4 9 5 0 0 0	3 3 7 5 0 0				
BALANCE SHEET						
Cash	8 0 0 0 0	5 0 0 0 0				
Accounts Receivable	2 1 3 0 0 0	1 1 2 5 0 0				
Inventory	1 4 0 0 0 0	1 1 5 0 0 0				
Investment in Sells Company	4 2 0 0 0 0					
Other Assets	5 9 9 0 0 0	6 3 0 0 0 0				
Total Assets	1 4 5 2 0 0 0	9 0 7 5 0 0				
Deferred Tax Liability	5 2 0 0 0	1 5 0 0 0				
Accounts Payable	7 0 0 0 0	3 0 0 0 0				
Other Liabilities	3 5 0 0 0	2 5 0 0 0				
Capital Stock						
Penta Company	8 0 0 0 0 0					
Sells Company		5 0 0 0 0 0				
Retained Earnings from Above	4 9 5 0 0 0	3 3 7 5 0 0				
Minority Interest in Net Assets						
Total Liabilities & Equity	1 4 5 2 0 0 0	9 0 7 5 0 0				

Copyright © 1991 by John Wiley & Sons, Inc.

NAME

SECTION

DATE

PERCY COMPANY AND SUBSIDIARY
Consolidated Statements Workpaper
For the Year Ended December 31, 1992

	Percy Company	Samatros Company	Eliminations Debit	Eliminations Credit	Minority Interest	Consolidated Balances
INCOME STATEMENT						
Sales	1100000	530000				
Dividend Income	7000					
Total Revenue	1107000	530000				
Cost of Goods Sold:						
Beginning Inventory	150000	110000				
Purchases	850000	350000				
Cost of Goods Available	1000000	460000				
Less Ending Inventory	140000	115000				
Cost of Goods Sold	860000	345000				
Income Tax Expense	27000	28250				
Other Expenses	180000	114000				
Total Cost and Expense	1067000	487250				
Net/Combined Income	40000	42750				
Minority Interest in Income						
Net Income to Retained Earnings	40000	42750				
STATEMENT OF RETAINED EARNINGS						
1/1 Retained Earnings						
Percy Company	541000					
Samatros Company		120000				

	Percy Company	Samatros Company	Eliminations Debit	Eliminations Credit	Minority Interest	Consolidated Balances
Net Income from Above	40000	42750				
Dividends Declared						
Percy Company	(100000)					
Samatros Company		(10000)				
12/31 Retained Earnings to						
Balance Sheet	481000	152750				
BALANCE SHEET						
Cash	35000	100000				
Accounts Receivable	211000	107750				
Inventory	140000	115000				
Investment in Samatros Company	420000					
Other Assets	500000	400000				
Total Assets	1306000	722750				
Accounts Payable	70000	30000				
Other Liabilities	55000	35000				
Deferred Income Tax Liability	20000	5000				
Capital Stock						
Percy Company	680000					
Samatros Company		500000				
Retained Earnings from Above	481000	152750				
Minority Interest in Net Assets						
Total Liabilities & Equity	1306000	722750				

NAME

SECTION

DATE

PENTA COMPANY AND SUBSIDIARY
Consolidated Statements Workpaper
For the Year Ended December 31, 1992

	Penta Company	Samatros Company	Eliminations Debit	Eliminations Credit	Consolidated Income Statement	Consolidated Retained Earnings Statement	Minority Interest	Consolidated Balance Sheet
DEBITS								
Cash	35000	100000						
Accounts Receivable (net)	211000	107750						
Inventory 1/1	150000	110000						
Investment in Samatros Company	420000							
Other Assets	500000	400000						
Dividends Declared								
Penta Company	100000							
Samatros Company		10000						
Purchases	850000	350000						
Other Expenses	180000	114000						
Income Tax Expense	27000	28250						
Totals	2473000	1220000						
Inventory 12/31	140000	115000						
Total Assets								

	Penta Company	Samatros Company	Eliminations Debit	Eliminations Credit	Consolidated Income Statement	Consolidated Retained Earnings Statement	Minority Interest	Consolidated Balance Sheet
CREDITS								
Accounts Payable	70000	30000						
Other Liabilities	55000	35000						
Deferred Income Tax Liability	20000	5000						
Common Stock								
Penta Company	680000							
Samatros Company		500000						
Retained Earnings								
Penta Company	541000							
Samatros Company		120000						
Sales	1100000	530000						
Dividend Income	7000							
Totals	2473000	1220000						
Inventory 12/31	140000	115000						
Net/Combined Income								
Minority Interest in Income								
Consolidated Net Income								
Consolidated Retained Earnings								
Minority Interest in Net Assets								
Total Liabilities and Equity								

NAME

SECTION

DATE

PLATT COMPANY AND SUBSIDIARY
Consolidated Statement Workpaper
For the Year Ended December 31, 1992

	Platt Company	Shelby Company	Eliminations Debit	Eliminations Credit	Minority Interest	Consolidated Balances
INCOME STATEMENT						
Sales	1 4 7 5 0 0 0	1 1 1 0 0 0 0				
Dividend Income	8 0 0 0 0					
Total Revenue	1 5 5 5 0 0 0	1 1 1 0 0 0 0				
Cost of Goods Sold	9 4 2 0 0 0	7 9 5 0 0 0				
Income Tax Expense	1 8 7 2 0 0	9 0 0 0 0				
Other Expenses	1 4 5 0 0 0	9 0 0 0 0				
Total Cost and Expense	1 2 7 4 2 0 0	9 7 5 0 0 0				
Net/Combined Income	2 8 0 8 0 0	1 3 5 0 0 0				
Minority Interest in Income						
Net Income to Retained Earnings	2 8 0 8 0 0	1 3 5 0 0 0				
STATEMENT OF RETAINED EARNINGS						
1/1 Retained Earnings:						
Platt Company	1 3 0 0 0 0 0					
Shelby Company		1 0 4 0 0 0 0				
Net Income from Above	2 8 0 8 0 0	1 3 5 0 0 0				
Dividends Declared:						
Platt Company	(1 2 0 0 0 0)					
Shelby Company		(1 0 0 0 0 0)				
12/31 Retained Earnings to Balance Sheet	1 4 6 0 8 0 0	1 0 7 5 0 0 0				

BALANCE SHEET	Platt Company	Shelby Company	Eliminations Debit	Eliminations Credit	Minority Interest	Consolidated Balances
Current Assets	568000	271000				
Investment in Shelby Company	1600000					
Plant and equipment	1972000	830000				
Accumulated Depreciation	(375000)	(290000)				
Other Assets	1068800	1600000				
Total Assets	4833800	2411000				
Deferred Tax Liability	168000	126000				
Other Liabilities	205000	10000				
Capital Stock						
Platt Company	3000000					
Shelby Company		1200000				
Retained Earnings from Above	1460800	1075000				
Minority Interest in Net Assets						
Total Liabilities & Equity	4833800	2411000				

NAME

SECTION

DATE

PIPE COMPANY AND SUBSIDIARY
Consolidated Statements Workpaper
For the Year Ended December 31, 1992

	Pipe Company	Shaw Company	Eliminations Debit	Eliminations Credit	Minority Interest	Consolidated Balances
INCOME STATEMENT						
Sales	1 8 6 0 0 0 0	9 9 0 0 0 0				
Gain on Sale of Equipment		9 0 0 0 0				
Dividend Income	1 4 0 0 0					
Total Revenue	1 8 7 4 0 0 0	1 0 8 0 0 0 0				
Cost of Goods Sold	1 0 3 7 0 0 0	4 0 0 0 0 0				
Depreciation Expense	7 0 0 0 0	5 0 0 0 0				
Other Expenses	3 2 2 0 0 0	1 0 0 0 0 0				
Income Tax Expense	1 7 8 0 0 0	2 1 0 0 0 0				
Total Cost and Expense	1 6 0 7 0 0 0	7 6 0 0 0 0				
Net/Combined Income	2 6 7 0 0 0	3 2 0 0 0 0				
Minority Interest in Income						
Net Income to Retained Earnings	2 6 7 0 0 0	3 2 0 0 0 0				
STATEMENT OF RETAINED EARNINGS						
1/1 Retained Earnings						
Pipe Company	7 8 0 0 0 0					

NAME _____

SECTION _____

DATE _____

	Pipe Company	Shaw Company	Eliminations Debit	Eliminations Credit	Minority Interest	Consolidated Balances
Shaw Company		2 6 0 0 0 0				
Net Income from Above	2 6 7 0 0 0	3 2 0 0 0 0				
Dividends Declared						
Pipe Company	(4 0 0 0 0)					
Shaw Company		(2 0 0 0 0)				
12/31 Retained Earnings to						
Balance Sheet	1 0 0 7 0 0 0	5 6 0 0 0 0				
BALANCE SHEET						
Cash	2 5 0 0 0 0	1 0 0 0 0 0				
Accounts Receivable	5 0 0 0 0 0	3 0 0 0 0 0				
Inventory	4 0 0 0 0 0	2 0 0 0 0 0				
Investment in Shaw Company	1 0 0 0 0 0 0					
Difference between Cost and Book Value						
Land	7 0 0 0 0 0	6 0 0 0 0 0				
Plant and Equipment	1 2 0 0 0 0 0	9 0 0 0 0 0				
Accumulated Depreciation	(4 2 3 0 0 0)	(3 5 0 0 0 0)				
Unamortized Excess of Cost Over F.V.						
Total Assets	3 6 2 7 0 0 0	1 7 5 0 0 0 0				
(Continued on next page)						

NAME

SECTION

DATE

	Pipe Company	Shaw Company	Eliminations Debit	Eliminations Credit	Minority Interest	Consolidated Balances
Current Liabilities	420000	30000				
Deferred Income Tax Liability	100000	60000				
Notes Payable	500000	200000				
Capital Stock						
Pipe Company	1600000					
Shaw Company		900000				
Retained Earnings from Above	1007000	560000				
Minority Interest in Net Assets						
Total Liabilities & Equity	3627000	1750000				

NAME

SECTION

DATE

PIPE COMPANY AND SUBSIDIARY
Consolidated Statements Workpaper
For the Year Ended December 31, 1993

	Pipe Company	Shaw Company	Eliminations Debit	Eliminations Credit	Consolidated Income Statement	Consolidated Retained Earnings Statement	Minority Interest	Consolidated Balance Sheet
DEBITS								
Cash	250000	100000						
Accounts Receivable	500000	300000						
Inventory	400000	200000						
Investment in Shaw Company	1000000							
Plant and Equipment	1200000	900000						
Accumulated Depreciation	(423000)	(350000)						
Difference between Cost and Book Value								
Unamortized Excess of Cost over Fair Value								
Land	700000	600000						
Cost of Goods Sold	1037000	400000						
Depreciation Expense	70000	500000						
Other Expenses	322000	100000						
Income Tax Expense	178000	210000						
(Continued on next page)								

NAME

SECTION

DATE

	Pipe Company	Shaw Company	Eliminations Debit	Eliminations Credit	Consolidated Income Statement	Consolidated Retained Earnings Statement	Minority Interest	Consolidated Balance Sheet
Dividends Declared								
Pipe Company	40000							
Shaw Company		20000						
Totals	5274000	2530000						
Total Assets								
CREDITS								
Current Liabilities	420000	300000						
Deferred Income Tax Liability	100000	600000						
Notes Payable	500000	200000						
Common Stock								
Pipe Company	1600000							
Shaw Company		900000						
Retained Earnings								
Pipe Company	780000							
Shaw Company		260000						
Sales	1860000	990000						
Gain on Sale of Equipment		90000						

	Pipe Company	Shaw Company	Eliminations Debit	Eliminations Credit	Consolidated Income Statement	Consolidated Retained Earnings Statement	Minority Interest	Consolidated Balance Sheet
Dividend Income	14000							
Totals	5274000	2530000						
Net/Combined Income								
Minority Interest in Income								
Consolidated Net Income								
Consolidated Retained Earnings								
Minority Interest in Net Assets								
Total Liabilities and Equity								

NAME

SECTION

DATE

PIPER COMPANY AND SUBSIDIARY
Consolidated Statements Workpaper
For the Year Ended December 31, 1992

	Piper Company	Savin Company	Eliminations Debit	Eliminations Credit	Minority Interest	Consolidated Balances
INCOME STATEMENT						
Sales	11 0 0 0 0 0	5 3 0 0 0 0				
Equity in Subsidiary Income	3 3 2 5 0					
Total Revenue	11 3 3 2 5 0	5 3 0 0 0 0				
Cost of Goods Sold:						
Beginning Inventory	1 5 0 0 0 0	1 1 0 0 0 0				
Purchases	8 5 0 0 0 0	3 5 0 0 0 0				
Cost of Goods Available	10 0 0 0 0 0	4 6 0 0 0 0				
Less Ending Inventory	1 4 0 0 0 0	1 1 5 0 0 0				
Cost of Goods Sold	8 6 0 0 0 0	3 4 5 0 0 0				
Income Tax Expense	3 2 0 0 0	2 0 5 0 0				
Other Expenses	1 7 5 0 0 0	1 1 7 0 0 0				
Total Cost and Expense	10 6 7 0 0 0	4 8 2 5 0 0				
Net/Combined Income	6 6 2 5 0	4 7 5 0 0				
Minority Interest in Income						
Net Income to Retained Earnings	6 6 2 5 0	4 7 5 0 0				
STATEMENT OF RETAINED EARNINGS						
1/1 Retained Earnings:						
Piper Company	6 9 5 0 0 0					
Savin Company		3 2 0 0 0 0				
Net Income from Above	6 6 2 5 0	4 7 5 0 0				

	Piper Company	Savin Company	Eliminations Debit	Eliminations Credit	Minority Interest	Consolidated Balances
Dividends Declared:						
Piper Company	(100000)					
Savin Company		(30000)				
12/31 Retained Earnings to						
Balance Sheet	661250	337500				
BALANCE SHEET						
Cash	80000	50000				
Accounts Receivable	213000	112500				
Inventory	140000	115000				
Investment in Savin Company	586250					
Other Assets	599000	630000				
Total Assets	1618250	907500				
Deferred Tax Liability	52000	15000				
Accounts Payable	70000	30000				
Other Liabilities	35000	25000				
Capital Stock						
Piper Company	800000					
Savin Company		500000				
Retained Earnings from Above	661250	337500				
Minority Interest in Net Assets						
Total Liabilities & Equity	1618250	907500				

NAME
SECTION
DATE

PETRA COMPANY AND SUBSIDIARY
Consolidated Statements Workpaper
For the Year Ended December 31, 1992

	Petra Company	Swain Company	Eliminations Debit	Eliminations Credit	Minority Interest	Consolidated Balances
INCOME STATEMENT						
Sales	1 100 000	530 000				
Equity in Subsidiary Income	29 925					
Total Revenue	1 129 925	530 000				
Cost of Goods Sold:						
Beginning Inventory	150 000	110 000				
Purchases	850 000	350 000				
Cost of Goods Available	1 000 000	460 000				
Less Ending Inventory	140 000	115 000				
Cost of Goods Sold	860 000	345 000				
Income Tax Expense	27 000	28 250				
Other Expenses	180 000	114 000				
Total Cost and Expense	1 067 000	487 250				
Net/Combined Income	62 925	42 750				
Minority Interest in Income						
Net Income to Retained Earnings	62 925	42 750				
STATEMENT OF RETAINED EARNINGS						
1/1 Retained Earnings:						
Petra Company	555 000					
Swain Company		120 000				
Net Income from Above	62 925	42 750				

NAME

SECTION

DATE

	Petra Company	Swain Company	Eliminations Debit	Eliminations Credit	Minority Interest	Consolidated Balances
Dividends Declared:						
Petra Company	(100000)					
Swain Company		(10000)				
12/31 Retained Earnings to						
Balance Sheet	517925	152750				
BALANCE SHEET						
Cash	35000	100000				
Accounts Receivable (net)	211000	107750				
Inventory	140000	115000				
Investment in Swain Company	456925					
Other Assets	500000	400000				
Total Assets	1342925	722750				
Accounts Payable	70000	30000				
Other Liabilities	55000	35000				
Deferred Income Tax Liability	20000	5000				
Capital Stock						
Petra Company	680000					
Swain Company		500000				
Retained Earnings from Above	517925	152750				
Minority Interest in Net Assets						
Total Liabilities & Equity	1342925	722750				

NAME

SECTION

DATE

PEREZ COMPANY AND SUBSIDIARY
Consolidated Statements Workpaper
For the Year Ended December 31, 1992

	Perez Company	Salars Company	Eliminations Debit	Eliminations Credit	Minority Interest	Consolidated Balances
INCOME STATEMENT						
Sales	1 4 7 5 0 0 0	1 1 1 0 0 0 0				
Equity in Subsidiary Income	1 0 8 0 0 0					
Total Revenue	1 5 8 3 0 0 0	1 1 1 0 0 0 0				
Cost of Goods Sold	9 4 2 0 0 0	7 9 5 0 0 0				
Income Tax Expense	1 8 7 2 0 0	9 0 0 0 0				
Other Expenses	1 4 5 0 0 0	9 0 0 0 0				
Total Cost and Expense	1 2 7 4 2 0 0	9 7 5 0 0 0				
Net/Combined Income	3 0 8 8 0 0	1 3 5 0 0 0				
Minority Interest in Income						
Net Income to Retained Earnings	3 0 8 8 0 0	1 3 5 0 0 0				
STATEMENT OF RETAINED EARNINGS						
1/1 Retained Earnings:						
Perez Company	1 4 9 2 0 0 0					
Salars Company		1 0 4 0 0 0 0				
Net Income from Above	3 0 8 8 0 0	1 3 5 0 0 0				
Dividends Declared:						
Perez Company	(1 2 0 0 0 0)					
Salars Company		(1 0 0 0 0 0)				
12/31 Retained Earnings to Balance Sheet	1 6 8 0 8 0 0	1 0 7 5 0 0 0				

BALANCE SHEET	Perez Company	Salars Company	Eliminations Debit	Eliminations Credit	Minority Interest	Consolidated Balances
Cash	5 6 8 0 0 0	2 7 1 0 0 0				
Investment in Salars Company	1 8 2 0 0 0 0					
Plant and Equipment	1 9 7 2 0 0 0	8 3 0 0 0 0				
Accumulated Depreciation	(3 7 5 0 0 0)	(2 9 0 0 0 0)				
Other Assets	1 0 6 8 8 0 0	1 6 0 0 0 0 0				
Total Assets	5 0 5 3 8 0 0	2 4 1 1 0 0 0				
Deferred Tax Liability	1 6 8 0 0 0	1 2 6 0 0 0				
Other Liabilities	2 0 5 0 0 0	1 0 0 0 0				
Capital Stock						
Perez Company	3 0 0 0 0 0 0					
Salars Company		1 2 0 0 0 0 0				
Retained Earnings from Above	1 6 8 0 8 0 0	1 0 7 5 0 0 0				
Minority Interest in Net Assets						
Total Liabilities & Equity	5 0 5 3 8 0 0	2 4 1 1 0 0 0				

NAME _____

SECTION _____

DATE _____

PEAK COMPANY AND SUBSIDIARY
Consolidated Statements Workpaper
For the Year Ended December 31, 1992

	Peak Company	Sill Company	Eliminations Debit	Eliminations Credit	Minority Interest	Consolidated Balances
INCOME STATEMENT						
Sales	1 9 4 0 0 0 0	8 0 0 0 0 0				
Dividend Income	7 2 0 0 0					
Total Revenue	2 0 1 2 0 0 0	8 0 0 0 0 0				
Cost of Goods Sold	1 2 2 0 0 0 0	5 2 0 0 0 0				
Other Expenses	3 8 0 0 0 0	1 1 0 0 0 0				
Total Cost and Expense	1 6 0 0 0 0 0	6 3 0 0 0 0				
Net/Combined Income	4 1 2 0 0 0	1 7 0 0 0 0				
Minority Interest in Income						
Net Income to Retained Earnings	4 1 2 0 0 0	1 7 0 0 0 0				
STATEMENT OF RETAINED EARNINGS						
1/1 Retained Earnings:						
Peak Company	7 2 0 0 0 0					
Sill Company		2 2 0 0 0 0				
Net Income from Above	4 1 2 0 0 0	1 7 0 0 0 0				
Dividends Declared:						
Peak Company	(1 6 0 0 0 0)					
Sill Company		(8 0 0 0 0)				
12/31 Retained Earnings to Balance Sheet	9 7 2 0 0 0	3 1 0 0 0 0				

	Peak Company	Sill Company	Eliminations Debit	Eliminations Credit	Minority Interest	Consolidated Balances
BALANCE SHEET						
Current Assets	291500	178000				
Investment in Sill Company	568500					
Other Assets	1080000	596000				
Total	1940000	774000				
Liabilities	168000	64000				
Capital Stock:						
Peak Company	800000					
Sill Company		400000				
Retained Earnings from Above	972000	310000				
Minority Interest in Net Assets						
Total Liabilities & Equity	1940000	774000				

NAME

SECTION

DATE

PLATE COMPANY AND SUBSIDIARY
Consolidated Statements Workpaper
For the Year Ended December 31, 1992

	Plate Company	Saucer Company	Eliminations Debit	Eliminations Credit	Minority Interest	Consolidated Balances
INCOME STATEMENT						
Income before Dividend						
Income and Gain on Sale*	1 7 9 0 0 0	1 8 2 0 0 0				
Dividend Income	2 1 0 0 0					
Gain on Sale of Investment	6 0 0 0 0					
Net/Combined Income	2 6 0 0 0 0	1 8 2 0 0 0				
Subsidiary Income Sold						
Minority Interest in Income						
Net Income to Retained Earnings	2 6 0 0 0 0	1 8 2 0 0 0				
RETAINED EARNINGS STATEMENT						
Retained Earnings, 1/1:						
Plate Company	1 6 5 0 0 0 0					
Saucer Company		4 0 0 0 0 0				
Net Income from Above	2 6 0 0 0 0	1 8 2 0 0 0				
Dividends Declared:						
Plate Company	(4 0 0 0 0)					
Saucer Company		(3 0 0 0 0)				
12/31 Retained Earnings to Balance Sheet	1 8 7 0 0 0 0	5 5 2 0 0 0				

NAME

SECTION

DATE

	Plate Company	Saucer Company	Eliminations Debit	Eliminations Credit	Minority Interest	Consolidated Balances
*Reported Net Income	$260000					
Less: Dividend Income .7($30,000)	(21000)					
Gain on Sale of Investment	(60000)					
$120,000 – .125($480,000)	$179000					
BALANCE SHEET						
Current Assets	900000	520000				
Investment in Saucer Company	420000					
Other Assets	1700000	592000				
Total	3020000	1112000				
Liabilities	390000	160000				
Common Stock:						
Plate Company	600000					
Saucer Company		250000				
Other Contributed capital:						
Plate Company	160000					
Saucer Company		150000				
Retained Earnings from Above	1870000	552000				
Minority Interest in Net Assets						
Total Liabilities & Equity	3020000	1112000				

ADULT COMPANY AND SUBSIDIARIES
Consolidated Statements Workpaper
December 31, 1992

	Adult Company	Baby Company	Child Company	Eliminations		Minority Interest	Consolidated Balances
				Debit	Credit		
INCOME STATEMENT							
Income from Independent Operations	60000	60000	60000				
Minority Interest in Income							
Net Income to Retained Earnings	60000	60000	60000				
RETAINED EARNINGS STATMENT							
1/1 Retained Earnings							
Adult Company	380000						
Baby Company		140000					
Child Company			100000				
Net Income from Above	60000	60000	60000				
12/31 Retained Earnings to							
Balance Sheet	440000	200000	160000				

NAME

SECTION

DATE

	Adult Company	Baby Company	Child Company	Eliminations Debit	Eliminations Credit	Minority Interest	Consolidated Balances
BALANCE SHEET							
Investment in Baby Company	455000						
Investment in Child Company	186000						
Investment in Child Company		49500					
Land							
～							
Common Stock:							
Adult Company	800000						
Baby Company		400000					
Child Company			200000				
Retained Earnings from Above	440000	200000	160000				
Minority Interest in Net Assets							

Copyright © 1991 by John Wiley & Sons, Inc.

NAME

SECTION

DATE

PUTTER COMPANY AND SUBSIDIARY
Consolidated Statements Workpaper
For the Year Ended December 31, 1993

	Putter Company	Stroke Company	Eliminations Debit	Eliminations Credit	Minority Interest	Consolidated Balances
INCOME STATEMENT						
Sales	300000	125000				
Dividend Income	12000	2500				
Total Revenue	312000	127500				
Cost of Sales and Expenses	220000	95000				
Net/Combined Income	92000	32500				
Minority Interest in Income						
Net Income to Retained Earnings	92000	32500				
RETAINED EARNINGS STATEMENT						
1/1 Retained Earnings:						
Putter Company	140000					
Stroke Company		60000				
Net Income from Above	92000	32500				
Dividends Declared:						
Putter Company	(25000)					
Stroke Company		(15000)				
12/31 Retained Earnings to Balance Sheet	207000	77500				

BALANCE SHEET	Putter Company	Stroke Company	Eliminations Debit	Eliminations Credit	Minority Interest	Consolidated Balances
Assets	2 8 2 0 0 0	1 2 1 2 5 0				
Investment in Stroke Company	6 8 0 0 0					
Investment in Putter Company		1 2 5 0 0				
Total	3 5 0 0 0 0	1 3 3 7 5 0				
Liabilities	4 3 0 0 0	3 1 2 5 0				
Common Stock:						
Putter Company	1 0 0 0 0 0					
Stroke Company		2 5 0 0 0				
Retained Earnings from Above	2 0 7 0 0 0	7 7 5 0 0				
Minority Interest in Net Assets						
Total Liabilities & Equity	3 5 0 0 0 0	1 3 3 7 5 0				

NAME

SECTION

DATE

A COMPANY AND SUBSIDIARIES
Consolidated Statements Workpaper
December 31, 1992

	A Company	B Company	C Company	Eliminations Debit	Eliminations Credit	Minority Interest	Consolidated Balances
ASSETS							
Current Assets	693600	440200	420600				
Investment in B Company	1135000						
Investment in C Company	75000						
Investment in C Company		590000					
Other Assets	1441400	680200	785000				
Total	3345000	1710400	1205600				
EQUITIES							
Liabilities	988800	494400	413800				
Capital Stock - A Company	1200000						
B Company		600000					
C Company			400000				
Other Contributed Capital - A Company	381200						
B Company		174800					
C Company			205000				
Retained Earnings - A Company	775000						
B Company		441200					
C Company			186800				
Minority Interest in Net Assets							
Total	3345000	1710400	1205600				

PLAY COMPANY AND SUBSIDIARY
Consolidated Statements Workpaper
For the Year Ended December 31, 1992

	Play Company	Sport Company	Eliminations Debit	Eliminations Credit	Minority Interest	Consolidated Balances
INCOME STATEMENT						
Sales	3 0 0 0 0 0	1 2 5 0 0 0				
Dividend Income	1 2 7 5 0	3 7 5 0				
Total Revenue	3 1 2 7 5 0	1 2 8 7 5 0				
Cost of Sales and Expenses	2 2 0 0 0 0	9 5 0 0 0				
Net/Combined Income	9 2 7 5 0	3 3 7 5 0				
Minority Interest in Income						
Net Income to Retained Earnings	9 2 7 5 0	3 3 7 5 0				
RETAINED EARNINGS STATEMENT						
1/1 Retained Earnings:						
Play Company	1 4 0 0 0 0					
Sport Company		6 0 0 0 0				
Net Income from Above	9 2 7 5 0	3 3 7 5 0				
Dividends Declared:						
Play Company	(2 5 0 0 0)					
Sport Company		(1 5 0 0 0)				
12/31 Retained Earnings to						
Balance Sheet	2 0 7 7 5 0	7 8 7 5 0				

NAME

SECTION

DATE

	Play Company	Sport Company	Eliminations Debit	Eliminations Credit	Minority Interest	Consolidated Balances
BALANCE SHEET						
Assets	284750	116250				
Investment in Sport Company	72250					
Investment in Play Company		15000				
Total	357000	131250				
Liabilities	49250	27500				
Capital Stock						
Play Company	100000					
Sport Company		25000				
Retained Earnings from Above	207750	78750				
Minority Interest in Net Assets						
Total Liabilities & Equity	357000	131250				

PUTTER COMPANY AND SUBSIDIARY
Consolidated Statements Workpaper
For the Year Ended December 31, 1993

	Putter Company	Stroke Company	Eliminations Debit	Eliminations Credit	Minority Interest	Consolidated Balances
INCOME STATEMENT						
Sales	300000	125000				
Dividend Income	22000	2500				
Equity in Subsidiary Income						
Total Revenue	322000	127500				
Cost of Sales and Expenses	220000	95000				
Net/Combined Income	102000	32500				
Minority Interest in Income						
Net Income to Retained Earnings	102000	32500				
RETAINED EARNINGS STATEMENT						
1/1 Retained Earnings:						
Putter Company	140000					
Stroke Company		60000				
Net Income from Above	102000	32500				
Dividends Declared:						
Putter Company	(25000)					
Stroke Company		(15000)				
12/31 Retained Earnings to						
Balance Sheet	217000	77500				

NAME _____

SECTION _____

DATE _____

	Putter Company	Stroke Company	Eliminations Debit	Eliminations Credit	Minority Interest	Consolidated Balances
BALANCE SHEET						
Assets	282000	121250				
Investment in Stroke Company	78000					
Investment in Putter Company		12500				
Total	360000	133750				
Liabilities	43000	31250				
Common Stock:						
Putter Company	100000					
Stroke Company		25000				
Retained Earnings from Above	217000	77500				
Minority Interest in Net Assets						
Total	360000	133750				

NAME

SECTION

DATE

B.

SPILMAN COMPANY AND SUBSIDIARY
Consolidated Statements Workpaper
For the Year Ended December 31, 1992

	Spilman Company	Yeager Company	Eliminations Debit	Eliminations Credit	Minority Interest	Consolidated Balances
INCOME STATEMENT						
Sales	2680000	1860000				
Dividend Income	160000					
Other Income	266000	120000				
Gain on Constructive						
Retirement of Bonds						
Total Revenue	3106000	1980000				
Expenses	2678000	1570000				
Net/Combined Income	428000	410000				
Minority Interest in Combined Income						
Net Income to Retained Earnings	428000	410000				
RETAINED EARNINGS STATEMENT						
1/1 Retained Earnings -						
Spilman Company	480000					
Yeager Company		300000				
Net Income from Above	428000	410000				
Dividends Declared -						
Spilman Company	(250000)					
Yeager Company		(200000)				
12/31 Retained Earnings to						
Balance Sheet	658000	510000				

B. (Continued)

BALANCE SHEET	Spilman Company	Yeager Company	Eliminations Debit	Eliminations Credit	Minority Interest	Consolidated Balances
Current Assets	9 2 0 0 0 0	5 8 0 0 0 0				
Investment in Yeager Company						
Common Stock	8 8 0 0 0 0					
Investment in Yeager Co. Bonds	3 5 3 4 0 0					
Other Assets	2 2 5 9 2 0 0	1 4 8 0 0 0 0				
Total Assets	4 4 1 2 6 0 0	2 0 6 0 0 0 0				
Bonds Payable	7 0 0 0 0 0	6 0 0 0 0 0				
Premium on Bonds Payable	2 0 0 0 0	9 0 0 0				
Other Liabilities	1 4 3 4 6 0 0	1 4 1 0 0 0				
Common Stock						
Spilman Company	1 6 0 0 0 0 0					
Yeager Company		8 0 0 0 0 0				
Retained Earnings from Above	6 5 8 0 0 0	5 1 0 0 0 0				
Minority Interest in Net Assets						
Total Liabilities and Equities	4 4 1 2 6 0 0	2 0 6 0 0 0 0				

NAME

SECTION

DATE

A.

SHORT COMPANY AND SUBSIDIARY
Consolidated Statements Workpaper
For the Year Ended December 31, 1992

	Short Company	Long Company	Eliminations Debit	Eliminations Credit	Minority Interest	Consolidated Balances
INCOME STATEMENT						
Sales	320000	200000				
Other Revenues	15000	2000				
Total Revenue	335000	202000				
Cost of Goods Sold	18000	110000				
Other Expenses	80000	30000				
Gain or Loss on Constructive						
Retirement of Bonds						
Total Cost & Expense	260000	140000				
Net/Combined Income	75000	62000				
Minority Interest in Income						
Net Income to Retained Earnings	75000	62000				
RETAINED EARNINGS STATEMENT						
1/1 Retained Earnings -						
Short Company	84000					
Long Company		65000				
Net Income from Above	75000	62000				
Dividends Declared -						
Short Company	(30000)					
Long Company - Stock Dividend		(50000)				
12/31 Retained Earnings to	129000	77000				
Balance Sheet						

A. (Continued)

BALANCE SHEET	Short Company	Long Company	Eliminations Debit	Eliminations Credit	Minority Interest	Consolidated Balances
Current Assets	1 2 5 0 0 0	1 4 8 0 0 0				
Investment in Long Company Stock	1 3 2 0 0 0					
Investment in Long Company Bonds	9 4 0 0 0					
Other Assets	3 0 0 0 0 0	3 1 5 0 0 0				
	6 5 1 0 0 0	4 6 3 0 0 0				
Accounts Payable	7 2 0 0 0	4 0 0 0 0				
Long-term Bonds Payable	2 5 0 0 0 0	2 0 0 0 0 0				
Discount on Bonds Payable		(4 0 0 0)				
Common Stock -						
Short Company	2 0 0 0 0 0					
Long Company		1 5 0 0 0 0				
Retained Earnings from Above	1 2 9 0 0 0	7 7 0 0 0				
Minority Interest in Net Assets	6 5 1 0 0 0	4 6 3 0 0 0				

NAME

SECTION

DATE

B.

PATTERSON COMPANY AND SUBSIDIARY
Consolidated Statements Workpaper
For the Year Ended December 31, 1992

	Patterson Company	Wilson Company	Eliminations Debit	Eliminations Credit	Minority Interest	Consolidated Balances
INCOME STATEMENT						
Sales	3 000 000	2 000 000				
Equity in Subsidiary Income	1 60 000					
Other Income	1 00 000	2 00 000				
Total Revenue	3 2 60 000	2 2 00 000				
Expenses	2 8 00 000	2 0 00 000				
Gain or Loss on Constructive						
Retirement of Bonds						
Net/Combined Income	4 60 000	2 00 000				
Minority Interest in Income						
Net Income to Retained Earnings	4 60 000	2 00 000				
RETAINED EARNINGS STATEMENT						
1/1 Retained Earnings -						
Patterson Company	6 00 000					
Wilson Company		3 00 000				
Net Income from Above	4 60 000	2 00 000				
Dividends Declared -						
Paterson Company	(2 5 0 000)					
Wilson Company		(1 00 000)				
12/31 Retained Earnings to						
Balance Sheet	8 1 0 000	4 00 000				

B. (Continued)

	Patterson Company	Wilson Company	Eliminations Debit	Eliminations Credit	Minority Interest	Consolidated Balances
BALANCE SHEET						
Current Assets	730000	700000				
Investment in Wilson Company						
Common Stock	1120000					
Investment in Wilson Co. Bonds	408000					
Other Assets	1252000	1400000				
Total Assets	3510000	2100000				
Bonds Payable	300000	500000				
Premium on Bonds Payable	20000	40000				
Other Liabilities	380000	160000				
Capital Stock						
Patterson Company	2000000					
Wilson Company		1000000				
Retained Earnings from Above	810000	400000				
Minority Interest in Net Assets						
Total Liabilities and Equities	3510000	2100000				

NAME _____

SECTION _____

DATE _____

RAM COMPANY AND SUBSIDIARY
Consolidated Statements Workpaper
For the Year Ended December 31, 1992

	Ram Company	Falcon Company	Eliminations Debit	Eliminations Credit	Minority Interest	Consolidated Balances
INCOME STATEMENT						
Sales	7 0 0 0 0 0	4 5 0 0 0 0				
Expenses	(5 8 0 0 0 0)	(3 5 0 0 0 0)				
Net Income	1 2 0 0 0 0	1 0 0 0 0 0				
Minority Interest in Income						
Preferred Stock						
Common Stock						
Net Income to Retained Earnings	1 2 0 0 0 0	1 0 0 0 0 0				
RETAINED EARNINGS STATEMENT						
1/1 Retained Earnings -						
Ram Company	5 0 7 0 0 0					
Falcon Company						
Preferred Stock		4 8 0 0 0 *				
Common Stock		3 8 2 0 0 0				
Net Income from Above	1 2 0 0 0 0	1 0 0 0 0 0				
Dividends Declared	(1 0 0 0 0 0)	- 0 -				
12/31 Retained Earnings to						
Balance Sheet	5 2 7 0 0 0	5 3 0 0 0 0				

*Dividends in arrears + call premium = ($400,000 × .10 × 1 year) + ($2 × 4,000 shares)

= $40,000 + 8,000

= $48,000

BALANCE SHEET	Ram Company	Falcon Company	Eliminations Debit	Eliminations Credit	Minority Interest	Consolidated Balances
Current Assets	1 5 7 8 0 0 0	8 9 0 0 0 0				
Investment - Common Stock	6 8 0 0 0 0					
Preferred Stock	1 7 5 0 0 0					
Other Assets	1 0 2 5 0 0 0	1 0 0 0 0 0 0				
	3 4 5 8 0 0 0	1 8 9 0 0 0 0				
Liabilities	9 3 1 0 0 0	3 6 0 0 0 0				
Preferred Stock						
Ram Company	4 0 0 0 0 0					
Falcon Company		4 0 0 0 0 0				
Common Stock						
Ram Company	1 0 0 0 0 0 0					
Falcon Company		5 0 0 0 0 0				
Other Contributed Capital						
Ram Company	6 0 0 0 0 0					
Falcon Company		1 0 0 0 0 0				
Retained Earnings from Above	5 2 7 0 0 0	5 3 0 0 0 0				
Minority Interest in Net Assets						
	3 4 5 8 0 0 0	1 8 9 0 0 0 0				

NAME

SECTION

DATE

B.

RAI COMPANY AND SUBSIDIARY
Consolidated Statements Workpaper
For the Year Ended December 31, 1992

	RAI Company	CO-OP Inc.	Eliminations Debit	Eliminations Credit	Minority Interest	Consolidated Balances
INCOME STATEMENT						
Sales	890000	750000				
Other Revenue	91000	50000				
Total Revenue	981000	800000				
Cost of Goods Sold	(500000)	(400000)				
Other Expenses	(330000)	(280000)				
Net/Combined Income	151000	120000				
Minority Interest in Income						
Preferred Stock						
Common Stock						
Net Income to Retained Earnings	151000	120000				
RETAINED EARNINGS STATEMENT						
1/1 Retained Earnings -						
RAI Company	560000					
CO-OP, Inc.		680000				
Preferred Stock		232000				
Common Stock		120000				
Net Income from Above	151000	120000				
Dividends Declared						
Preferred Stock		(26000)				
Common Stock		(64000)				
12/31 Retained Earnings to						
Balance Sheet	711000	330000				

NAME

SECTION

DATE

B. (Continued)

BALANCE SHEET	RAI Company	CO-OP Inc.	Eliminations Debit	Eliminations Credit	Minority Interest	Consolidated Balances
Current Assets	8 7 0 0 0 0	3 8 0 0 0 0				
Investment in CO-OP, Inc.						
Common Stock	5 5 0 0 0 0					
Preferred Stock	5 0 0 0 0					
Other Assets	1 2 7 6 0 0 0	6 0 0 0 0 0				
	2 7 4 6 0 0 0	9 8 0 0 0 0				
Liabilities	1 3 5 0 0 0	1 5 0 0 0 0				
Common Stock - RAI Company	7 0 0 0 0 0					
CO-OP, Inc.		4 0 0 0 0 0				
Preferred Stock		1 0 0 0 0 0				
Retained Earnings from Above	7 1 1 0 0 0	3 3 0 0 0 0				
Minority Interest						
	2 7 4 6 0 0 0	9 8 0 0 0 0				

NAME

SECTION

DATE

B.

PIONEER INDUSTRIES AND SUBSIDIARY
Consolidated Statements Workpaper
For the Year Ended December 31, 1992

	Pioneer Industries	Sugarloaf Company	Eliminations Debit	Eliminations Credit	Minority Interest	Consolidated Balances
INCOME STATEMENT						
Sales	4 0 4 0 0 0	3 0 0 0 0 0				
Dividend Income	8 0 0 0					
Total Revenue	4 1 2 0 0 0	3 0 0 0 0 0				
Cost of Goods Sold	2 0 0 0 0 0	1 6 0 0 0 0				
Operating Expenses	3 6 4 0 0	5 0 0 0 0				
Income Taxes	4 0 2 0 0	2 7 0 0 0				
Total Cost and Revenue	2 7 6 6 0 0	2 3 7 0 0 0				
Net/Combined Income	1 3 5 4 0 0	6 3 0 0 0				
Minority Interest in Income						
Preferred Stock						
Common Stock						
Net Income to Retained Earnings	1 3 5 4 0 0	6 3 0 0 0				
RETAINED EARNINGS STATEMENT						
1/1 Retained Earnings -						
Pioneer Industries	1 5 7 4 0 0					
Sugarloaf Company						
Preferred Stock		2 2 0 0 0				
Common Stock		8 5 0 0 0				
Net Income from Above	1 3 5 4 0 0	6 3 0 0 0				
(Continued on next page)						

NAME

SECTION

DATE

B. (Continued)

	Pioneer Industries	Sugarloaf Company	Eliminations Debit	Eliminations Credit	Minority Interest	Consolidated Balances
Dividends Declared						
Pioneer Industries	(6 5 0 0 0)					
Sugarloaf Company						
Preferred Stock		(3 0 0 0 0)				
Common Stock		(1 0 0 0 0)				
12/31 Retained Earningsk to						
Balance Sheet	2 2 7 8 0 0	1 3 0 0 0 0				
BALANCE SHEET						
Cash and Receivables	4 0 0 8 0 0	2 1 5 0 0 0				
Inventories	2 0 0 0 0 0	1 7 0 0 0 0				
Land	3 0 0 0 0 0	1 2 0 0 0 0				
Buildings and Equipment	6 9 7 0 0 0	2 4 5 0 0 0				
Accumulated Depreciation	(1 0 0 0 0 0)	(7 0 0 0 0)				
Investment in Sugarloaf Company	3 0 0 0 0 0					
Excess Cost over Fair Value						
Difference between Cost and						
Book Value	1 7 9 7 8 0 0	6 8 0 0 0 0				

NAME

SECTION

DATE

B. (Continued)

	Pioneer Industries	Sugarloaf Company	Eliminations Debit	Eliminations Credit	Minority Interest	Consolidated Balances
Current Liabilities	3 7 0 0 0 0	1 0 0 0 0 0				
Bonds Payable	4 0 0 0 0 0	1 0 0 0 0 0				
Common Stock						
Pioneer Industries, $10 par	6 0 0 0 0 0					
Sugarloaf Company, $10 par		2 0 0 0 0 0				
Preferred Stock - Sugarloaf Company		1 0 0 0 0 0				
Other Contributed Capital						
Pioneer Industries	2 0 0 0 0 0					
Sugarloaf Company		5 0 0 0 0				
Retained Earnings from Above	2 2 7 8 0 0	1 3 0 0 0 0				
Minority Interest in Net Assets						
	1 7 9 7 8 0 0	6 8 0 0 0 0				

NAME

SECTION

DATE

A. (1)

POWELL COMPANY AND SUBSIDIARY
Consolidated Statements Workpaper
100 Percent Elimination
For the Year Ended December 31, 1993

	Powell Company	Snell Company	Eliminations Debit	Eliminations Credit	Minority Interest	Consolidated Balances
INCOME STATEMENT						
Sales	400000	200000				
Dividend Income	4000					
Total Revenue	404000	200000				
Inventory—January 1	72000	32000				
Purchases	200000	104000				
Inventory—December 31	(96000)	(48000)				
Cost of Goods Sold	176000	88000				
Expenses	16000	8000				
Total Cost and Expense	192000	96000				
Net/Combined Income	212000	104000				
Minority Interest in Income						
Net	212000	104000				
RETAINED EARNINGS STATEMENT						
1/1/93 Retained Earnings:						
Powell Company	365900					
Snell Company		172000				
Net Income from Above	212000	104000				
Dividends Declared						
Powell Company	(40000)					
Snell Company		(5000)				
12/31/93 Retained Earnings	537900	271000				

A. (2)

POWELL COMPANY AND SUBSIDIARY
Consolidated Statements Workpaper
Partial Elimination
For the Year Ended December 31, 1993

	Powell Company	Snell Company	Eliminations Debit	Eliminations Credit	Minority Interest	Consolidated Balances
INCOME STATEMENT						
Sales	400000	200000				
Dividend Income	4000					
Total Revenue	404000	200000				
Inventory—January 1	72000	32000				
Purchases	200000	104000				
Inventory—December 31	(96000)	(48000)				
Cost of Goods Sold	176000	88000				
Expenses	16000	8000				
Total Cost and Expense	192000	96000				
Net/Combined Income	212000	104000				
Minority Interest in Income						
Net	212000	104000				
RETAINED EARNINGS STATEMENT						
1/1/93 Retained Earnings:						
Powell Company	365900					
Snell Company		172000				
Net Income from Above	212000	104000				
Dividends Declared						
Powell Company	(40000)					
Snell Company		(5000)				
12/31/93 Retained Earnings	537900	271000				

NAME

SECTION

DATE

B. Entity Theory

PURE COMPANY AND SUBSIDIARY
Consolidated Statements Workpaper
For the Year Ended December 31, 1992

	Pure Company	Simple Company	Eliminations Debit	Eliminations Credit	Minority Interest	Consolidated Balances
Sales	5 2 2 5 0 0	2 0 0 0 0 0				
Dividend Income	2 2 5 0 0					
Total Revenue	5 4 5 0 0 0	2 0 0 0 0 0				
Cost of Goods Sold	4 2 5 0 0 0	9 0 0 0 0				
Depreciation Expense						
Amortization of Goodwill						
Other Expense	5 0 0 0 0	3 5 0 0 0				
Total Cost and Expense	4 7 5 0 0 0	1 2 5 0 0 0				
Net/Combined Income	7 0 0 0 0	7 5 0 0 0				
Minority Interest in Income						
Net Income to Retained Earnings	7 0 0 0 0	7 5 0 0 0				
RETAINED EARNINGS STATEMENT						
1/1 Retained Earnings:						
Pure Company	2 4 0 0 0 0					
Simple Company		1 0 0 0 0 0				
Net Income from Above	7 0 0 0 0	7 5 0 0 0				
Dividends Declared:						
Pure Company	(5 0 0 0 0)					
Simple Company		(2 5 0 0 0)				
12/31 Retained Earnings to Balance Sheet	2 6 0 0 0 0	1 5 0 0 0 0				

NAME _____

SECTION _____

DATE _____

B. (Continued) Entity Theory

BALANCE SHEET	Pure Company	Simple Company	Eliminations Debit	Eliminations Credit	Minority Interest	Consolidated Balances
Cash	4 0 0 0 0	2 5 0 0 0				
Accounts Receivable	8 5 0 0 0	8 5 0 0 0				
Inventory	1 1 5 0 0 0	7 5 0 0 0				
Investment in Simple Company	4 5 0 0 0 0					
Difference Between Cost &						
Book Value						
Land		1 5 0 0 0 0				
Property and Equipment (net)	1 7 5 0 0 0	1 2 5 0 0 0				
Goodwill						
Total	8 6 5 0 0 0	4 6 0 0 0 0				
Accounts Payable	8 0 0 0 0	5 0 0 0 0				
Notes Payable	2 5 0 0 0	1 0 0 0 0				
Capital Stock						
Pure Company	5 0 0 0 0 0					
Simple Company		2 5 0 0 0 0				
Retained Earnings from Above	2 6 0 0 0 0	1 5 0 0 0 0				
Minority Interest in Net Assets						
Total	8 6 5 0 0 0	4 6 0 0 0 0				

NAME

SECTION

DATE

C. Parent Company Theory

PURE COMPANY AND SUBSIDIARY
Consolidated Statement Workpaper
For the Year Ended December 31, 1992

	Pure Company	Simple Company	Eliminations Debit	Eliminations Credit	Minority Interest	Consolidated Balances
Sales	5 2 2 5 0 0	2 0 0 0 0 0				
Dividend Income	2 2 5 0 0					
Total Revenue	5 4 5 0 0 0	2 0 0 0 0 0				
Cost of Goods Sold	4 2 5 0 0 0	9 0 0 0 0				
Depreciation Expense						
Amortization of Goodwill						
Other Expense	5 0 0 0 0	3 5 0 0 0				
Total Cost and Expense	4 7 5 0 0 0	1 2 5 0 0 0				
Net/Combined Income	7 0 0 0 0	7 5 0 0 0				
Minority Interest in Income						
Net Income to Retained Earnings	7 0 0 0 0	7 5 0 0 0				
RETAINED EARNINGS STATEMENT						
1/1 Retained Earnings:						
Pure Company	2 4 0 0 0 0					
Simple Company		1 0 0 0 0 0				
Net Income from Above	7 0 0 0 0	7 5 0 0 0				
Dividends Declared:						
Pure Company	(5 0 0 0 0)					
Simple Company		(2 5 0 0 0)				
12/31 Retained Earnings to Balance Sheet	2 6 0 0 0 0	1 5 0 0 0 0				

NAME

SECTION

DATE

C. (Continued) Parent Company Theory

BALANCE SHEET	Pure Company	Simple Company	Eliminations Debit	Eliminations Credit	Minority Interest	Consolidated Balances
Cash	4 0 0 0 0	2 5 0 0 0				
Accounts Receivable	8 5 0 0 0	8 5 0 0 0				
Inventory	1 1 5 0 0 0	7 5 0 0 0				
Investment in Simple Company	4 5 0 0 0 0					
Difference Between Cost &						
Book Value						
Land		1 5 0 0 0 0				
Property and Equipment (net)	1 7 5 0 0 0	1 2 5 0 0 0				
Goodwill						
Total	8 6 5 0 0 0	4 6 0 0 0 0				
Accounts Payable	8 0 0 0 0	5 0 0 0 0				
Notes Payable	2 5 0 0 0	1 0 0 0 0				
Capital Stock						
Pure Company	5 0 0 0 0 0					
Simple Company		2 5 0 0 0 0				
Retained Earnings from Above	2 6 0 0 0 0	1 5 0 0 0 0				
Minority Interest in Net Assets						
Total	8 6 5 0 0 0	4 6 0 0 0 0				

NAME

SECTION

DATE

B.

PEPPER COMPANY AND SUBSIDIARY
Consolidated Statements Workpaper
Partial Elimination
For the Year Ended December 31, 1992

	Pepper Company	Salt Company	Eliminations Debit	Eliminations Credit	Minority Interest	Consolidated Balances
INCOME STATEMENT						
Sales	550000	265000				
Dividend Income	27000					
Total Revenue	577000	265000				
Cost of Goods Sold:						
Inventory-1/1	75000	55000				
Purchases	425000	175000				
	500000	230000				
Inventory-12/31	70000	57500				
Cost of Goods Sold	430000	172500				
Other Expense	60000	45000				
Income Tax Expense	43500	23750				
Total Cost and Expense	533500	241250				
Net/Combined Income	43500	23750				
Minority Interest in Income						
Net Income to Retained Earnings	43500	23750				
RETAINED EARNINGS STATEMENT						
1/1 Retained Earnings:						
Pepper Company	270500					
Salt Company		60000				
Net Income from Above	43500	23750				

NAME

SECTION

DATE

B. (Continued)

	Pepper Company	Salt Company	Eliminations Debit	Eliminations Credit	Minority Interest	Consolidated Balances
Dividends Declared:						
Pepper Company	(5 0 0 0 0)					
Salt Company		(3 0 0 0 0)				
12/31 Retained Earnings to						
Balance Sheet	2 6 4 0 0 0	5 3 7 5 0				
BALANCE SHEET						
Cash	4 0 0 0 0	2 5 0 0 0				
Accounts Receivable (net)	1 0 6 5 0 0	5 6 2 5 0				
Inventory	7 0 0 0 0	5 7 5 0 0				
Investment in Salt Company	2 7 0 0 0 0					
Other Assets	2 5 0 0 0 0	2 0 0 0 0 0				
Total	7 3 6 5 0 0	3 3 8 7 5 0				
Accounts Payable	3 5 0 0 0	1 5 0 0 0				
Other Liabilities	3 7 5 0 0	2 0 0 0 0				
Common Stock						
Pepper Company	4 0 0 0 0 0					
Salt Company		2 5 0 0 0 0				
Retained Earnings from Above	2 6 4 0 0 0	5 3 7 5 0				
Minority Interest in Net Assets						
Total	7 3 6 5 0 0	3 3 8 7 5 0				

PEPPER COMPANY AND SUBSIDIARY
Consolidated Statements Workpaper
100% Elimination
For the Year Ended December 31, 1992

	Pepper Company	Salt Company	Eliminations Debit	Eliminations Credit	Minority Interest	Consolidated Balances
INCOME STATEMENT						
Sales	5 5 0 0 0 0	2 6 5 0 0 0				
Dividend Income	2 7 0 0 0					
Total Revenue	5 7 7 0 0 0	2 6 5 0 0 0				
Cost of Goods Sold:						
Inventory-1/1	7 5 0 0 0	5 5 0 0 0				
Purchases	4 2 5 0 0 0	1 7 5 0 0 0				
	5 0 0 0 0 0	2 3 0 0 0 0				
Inventory-12/31	7 0 0 0 0	5 7 5 0 0				
Cost of Goods Sold	4 3 0 0 0 0	1 7 2 5 0 0				
Other Expense	6 0 0 0 0	4 5 0 0 0				
Income Tax Expense	4 3 5 0 0	2 3 7 5 0				
Total Cost and Expense	5 3 3 5 0 0	2 4 1 2 5 0				
Net/Combined Income	4 3 5 0 0	2 3 7 5 0				
Minority Interest in Income						
Net Income to Retained Earnings	4 3 5 0 0	2 3 7 5 0				
RETAINED EARNINGS STATEMENT						
1/1 Retained Earnings:						
Pepper Company	2 7 0 5 0 0					
Salt Company		6 0 0 0 0				
Net Income from Above	4 3 5 0 0	2 3 7 5 0				

NAME

SECTION

DATE

C. (Continued)

	Pepper Company	Salt Company	Eliminations Debit	Eliminations Credit	Minority Interest	Consolidated Balances
Dividends Declared:						
Pepper Company	(5 0 0 0 0)					
Salt Company		(3 0 0 0 0)				
12/31 Retained Earnings to						
Balance Sheet	2 6 4 0 0 0	5 3 7 5 0				
BALANCE SHEET						
Cash	4 0 0 0 0	2 5 0 0 0				
Accounts Receivable (net)	1 0 6 5 0 0	5 6 2 5 0				
Inventory	7 0 0 0 0	5 7 5 0 0				
Investment in Salt Company	2 7 0 0 0 0					
Other Assets	2 5 0 0 0 0	2 0 0 0 0 0				
Total	7 3 6 5 0 0	3 3 8 7 5 0				
Accounts Payable	3 5 0 0 0	1 5 0 0 0				
Other Liabilities	3 7 5 0 0	2 0 0 0 0				
Common Stock						
Pepper Company	4 0 0 0 0 0					
Salt Company		2 5 0 0 0 0				
Retained Earnings from Above	2 6 4 0 0 0	5 3 7 5 0				
Minority Interest in Net Assets						
Total	7 3 6 5 0 0	3 3 8 7 5 0				

PARK COMPANY AND SUBSIDIARY
Consolidated Statements Workpaper
For the Year Ended December 31, 1992

	Park Company	Salem Company	Eliminations Debit	Eliminations Credit	Minority Interest	Consolidated Balances
INCOME STATEMENT						
Sales	1050000	400000				
Equity in Subsidiary Income	96000					
Total Revenue	1146000	400000				
Cost of Goods Sold	850000	180000				
Depreciation Expense	35000	25000				
Other Expenses	65000	45000				
Total Cost & Expense	950000	250000				
Net/Combined Income	196000	150000				
Minority Interest in Income						
Net Income to Retained Earnings	196000	150000				
STATEMENT OF RETAINED EARNINGS						
1/1 Retained Earnings						
Park Company	482000					
Salem Company		200000				
Net Income from Above	196000	150000				
Dividends Declared						
Park Company	(100000)					
Salem Company		(50000)				
12/31 Retained Earnings						
to Balance Sheet	578000	300000				

NAME

SECTION

DATE

BALANCE SHEET	Park Company	Salem Company	Eliminations Debit	Eliminations Credit	Minority Interest	Consolidated Balances
Cash	80000	50000				
Accounts Receivable	250000	170000				
Inventory	230000	150000				
Investment in Salem Company	878000					
Difference Between Cost and						
Book Value						
Land		300000				
Plant and Equipment (net)	350000	250000				
Unamortized Excess of Cost						
Over Fair Value						
Total Assets	1788000	920000				
Accounts Payable	160000	100000				
Notes Payable	50000	20000				
Capital Stock						
Park Company	1000000					
Salem Company		500000				
Retained Earnings from Above	578000	300000				
Minority Interest in Net Assets						
Total Liabilities & Equity	1788000	920000				

NAME

SECTION

DATE

PENNELL COMPANY AND SUBSIDIARY
Consolidated Statements Workpaper
For the Year Ended December 31, 1992

	Pennell Company	Segal Company	Eliminations Debit	Eliminations Credit	Minority Interest	Consolidated Balances
INCOME STATEMENT						
Sales	1 6 5 0 0 0 0	7 9 5 0 0 0				
Equity in Subsidiary Income	9 1 1 2 5					
Total Revenue	1 7 4 1 1 2 5	7 9 5 0 0 0				
Cost of Goods Sold:						
Beginning Inventory	2 2 5 0 0 0	1 6 5 0 0 0				
Purchases	1 2 7 5 0 0 0	5 2 5 0 0 0				
Cost of Goods Available	1 5 0 0 0 0 0	6 9 0 0 0 0				
Less Ending Inventory	2 1 0 0 0 0	1 7 2 5 0 0				
Cost of Goods Sold	1 2 9 0 0 0 0	5 1 7 5 0 0				
Other Expenses	3 1 0 5 0 0	2 0 6 2 5 0				
Total Cost & Expense	1 6 0 0 5 0 0	7 2 3 7 5 0				
Net/Combined Income	1 4 0 6 2 5	7 1 2 5 0				
Minority Interest in Income						
Net Income to Retained Earnings	1 4 0 6 2 5	7 1 2 5 0				
STATEMENT OF RETAINED EARNINGS						
1/1 Retained Earnings						
Pennell Company	7 9 8 0 0 0					
Segal Company		1 8 0 0 0 0				
Net Income from Above	1 4 0 6 2 5	7 1 2 5 0				

	Pennell Company	Segal Company	Eliminations Debit	Eliminations Credit	Minority Interest	Consolidated Balances
Dividends Declared						
Pennell Company	(150000)					
Segal Company		(90000)				
12/31 Retained Earnings						
to Balance Sheet	788625	161250				
BALANCE SHEET						
Cash	120000	75000				
Accounts Receivable	319500	168750				
Inventory	210000	172500				
Investment in Segal Company	806625					
Other Assets	750000	600000				
Total Assets	2206125	1016250				
Accounts Payable	105000	45000				
Other Liabilities	112500	60000				
Capital Stock						
Pennell Company	1200000					
Segal Company		750000				
Retained Earnings from Above	788625	161250				
Minority Interest in Net Assets						
Total Liabilities & Equity	2206125	1016250				

C.

PITTS COMPANY AND SUBSIDIARY
Consolidated Statements Workpaper
For the Year Ended December 31, 1993

	Pitts Company	Shannon Company	Eliminations Debit	Eliminations Credit	Minority Interest	Consolidated Balances
INCOME STATEMENT						
Sales	1950000	1350000				
Equity in Subsidiary Income	252000					
Total Revenue	2202000	1350000				
Cost of Goods Sold	1350000	900000				
Other Expenses	225000	150000				
Total Cost & Expense	1575000	1050000				
Net/Combined Income	627000	300000				
Minority Interest in Income						
Net Income to Retained Earnings	627000	300000				
STATEMENT OF RETAINED EARNINGS						
1/1 Retained Earnings						
Pitts Company	1397400					
Shannon Company		1038000				
Net Income from Above	627000	300000				
Dividends Declared						
Pitts Company	(150000)					
Shannon Company		(75000)				
12/31 Retained Earnings						
to Balance Sheet	1874400	1263000				

NAME
SECTION
DATE

C. (Continued)

	Pitts Company	Shannon Company	Eliminations Debit	Eliminations Credit	Minority Interest	Consolidated Balances
BALANCE SHEET						
Inventory	498000	225000				
Investment in Shannon Company	1334400					
Plant and Equipment	2168100	2625000				
Accumulated Depreciation	(900000)	(612000)				
Total Assets	3100500	2238000				
Liabilities	465600	450000				
Capital Stock						
Pitts Company	760500					
Shannon Company		525000				
Retained Earnings from Above	1874400	1263000				
Minority Interest in Net Assets						
Total Liabilities & Equity	3100500	2238000				

NAME

SECTION

DATE

C.

PINKARD COMPANY AND SUBSIDIARY
Consolidated Statements Workpaper
For the Year Ended December 31, 1992

	Pinkard Company	Sharp Company	Eliminations Debit	Eliminations Credit	Minority Interest	Consolidated Balances
INCOME STATEMENT						
Sales	1860000	990000				
Gain on Sale of Land		90000				
Equity in Subsidiary Income	150300					
Total Revenue	2010300	1080000				
Cost of Goods Sold	1037000	500000				
Depreciation Expense	70000	50000				
Other Expenses	300000	130000				
Tax Expense	121200	80000				
Total Cost & Expense	1528200	760000				
Net/Combined Income	482100	320000				
Minority Interest in Income						
Net Income to Retained Earnings	482100	320000				
STATEMENT OF RETAINED EARNINGS						
1/1 Retained Earnings						
Pinkard Company	700000					
Sharp Company		200000				
Net Income from Above	482100	320000				
Dividends Declared						
Pinkard Company	(40000)					
Sharp Company		(20000)				
12/31 Retained Earnings to Bal. Sheet	1142100	500000				

NAME

SECTION

DATE

C. (Continued)

BALANCE SHEET	Pinkard Company	Sharp Company	Eliminations Debit	Eliminations Credit	Minority Interest	Consolidated Balances
Cash	2 5 0 0 0 0	1 0 0 0 0 0				
Accounts Receivable	5 0 0 0 0 0	3 0 0 0 0 0				
Inventory	4 0 0 0 0 0	2 0 0 0 0 0				
Investment in Sharp Company	1 1 3 6 3 0 0					
Difference Between Cost and Book Value						
Land	7 0 0 0 0 0	6 0 0 0 0 0				
Plant and Equipment	1 2 0 0 0 0 0	9 0 0 0 0 0				
Accumulated Depreciation	(4 2 3 0 0 0)	(3 5 0 0 0 0)				
Unamortized Excess of Cost Over F.V.						
Total Assets	3 7 6 3 3 0 0	1 7 5 0 0 0 0				
Income Tax Payable	1 0 6 7 0 0	4 0 0 0 0				
Accounts Payable	3 0 0 0 0 0	5 0 0 0 0				
Deferred Tax Liability	1 1 4 5 0 0	6 0 0 0 0				
Notes Payable	5 0 0 0 0 0	2 0 0 0 0 0				
Capital Stock						
Pinkard Company	1 6 0 0 0 0 0					
Sharp Company		9 0 0 0 0 0				
Retained Earnings from Above	1 1 4 2 1 0 0	5 0 0 0 0 0				
Minority Interest in Net Assets						
Total Liabilities & Equity	3 7 6 3 3 0 0	1 7 5 0 0 0 0				

P COMPANY AND SUBSIDIARY
Consolidated Statements Workpaper
For the Year Ended December 31, 1993

	P Company	SFr Company	Eliminations Debit	Eliminations Credit	Minority Interest	Consolidated Balances
INCOME STATEMENT						
Sales	4 2 0 0 0 0 0	6 6 4 4 0 0				
Dividend Income	5 4 0 0 0					
Total Revenues	4 2 5 4 0 0 0	6 6 4 4 0 0				
Cost of Goods Sold	2 7 2 0 0 0 0	4 0 7 0 0 0				
Depreciation Expense	2 1 0 0 0 0	2 2 0 0 0				
Other Expense	9 1 4 0 0 0	1 4 4 1 0 0				
Income Tax Expense	1 0 0 0 0 0	1 8 0 4 0				
Total Expenses	3 9 4 4 0 0 0	5 9 1 1 4 0				
Net Income	3 1 0 0 0 0	7 3 2 6 0				
Minority Interest in Income						
Net Income to Retained Earnings	3 1 0 0 0 0	7 3 2 6 0				
RETAINED EARNINGS STATEMENT						
Retained Earnings - 1/1						
P Company	5 4 4 4 0 0					
SFr Company		7 5 9 4 8				
Net Income from Above	3 1 0 0 0 0	7 3 2 6 0				
Dividends Declared						
P Company	(2 0 0 0 0 0)					
SFr Comany		(6 7 5 0 0)				
Retained Earnings to						
Balance Sheet - 12/31	6 5 4 4 0 0	8 1 7 0 8				

NAME
SECTION
DATE

BALANCE SHEET	P Company	SFr Company	Eliminations Debit	Eliminations Credit	Minority Interest	Consolidated Balances
Cash	500200	182875				
Accounts Receivable	516400	125400				
Inventories (FIFO Cost)	627800	197125				
Investment in SFr Company	300000					
Land	450000	95000				
Building (net)	610000	104500				
Equipment (net)	290000	76950				
Difference between Cost and Book Value	- -	- -				
Total	3294400	781850				
Accounts Payable	540000	152000				
Short-term Notes Payable	300000	123643				
Bonds Payable	700000	161500				
Common Stock						
P Company	800000					
SFr Company		144000				
Additional Paid-In Capital						
P Company	300000					
SFr Company		45000				
Cumulative Translation Adjustment						
P Company	- - -					
SFr Company						
Retained Earnings	654400	73999				
		81708				
Minority Interest in Net Assets						
Total	3294400	781850				

NAME _____

SECTION _____

DATE _____

C.

P COMPANY AND SUBSIDIARY
Consolidated Statements Workpaper
For the Year Ended December 31, 1993

	P Company	SFr Company	Eliminations Debit	Eliminations Credit	Minority Interest	Consolidated Balances
INCOME STATEMENT						
Sales	4 2 0 0 0 0 0	6 6 4 4 0 0				
Dividend Income	5 4 0 0 0					
Total Revenues	4 2 5 4 0 0 0	6 6 4 4 0 0				
Cost of Goods Sold	2 7 2 0 0 0 0	3 8 8 5 3 2				
Depreciation Expense	2 1 0 0 0 0	1 8 7 5 0				
Other Expenses	9 1 4 0 0 0	1 4 4 1 0 0				
Income Tax Expense	1 0 0 0 0 0	1 8 0 4 0				
Total Expense	3 9 4 4 0 0 0	5 6 9 4 2 2				
Translation Loss	- - -	1 1 8 1 8				
Net Income	3 1 0 0 0 0	8 3 1 6 0				
Minority Interest in Income	- - -	- - -				
Net Income to Retained Earnings	3 1 0 0 0 0	8 3 1 6 0				
RETAINED EARNINGS STATMENT						
Retained Earnings - 1/1						
P Company	5 4 4 4 0 0					
SFr Company		7 6 6 6 0				
Net Income from Above	3 1 0 0 0 0	8 3 1 6 0				
Dividends Declared						
P Company	(2 0 0 0 0 0)					
SFr Company		(6 7 5 0 0)				
Retained Earnings to						
Balance Sheet - 12/31	6 5 4 4 0 0	9 2 3 2 0				

C. (Continued)

	P Company	SFr Company	Eliminations Debit	Eliminations Credit	Minority Interest	Consolidated Balances
BALANCE SHEET						
Cash	500200	182875				
Accounts Receivable	516400	125400				
Inventories	627800	191938				
Investment in SFr Company	300000					
Land	450000	75000				
Building (net)	610000	82500				
Equipment (net)	290000	60750				
Differece between Cost and						
Book Value	- -	- -				
Total Assets	3294400	718463				
Accounts Payable	540000	152000				
Short-term Notes Payable	300000	123643				
Bonds Payable	700000	161500				
Common Stock						
P Company	300000					
SFr Company		144000				
Additional Paid-In Capital						
P Company	800000					
SFr Company		45000				
Retained Earnings from Above	654400	92320				
Minority Interest in Net Assets						
Total Liabilities &						
Owner's Equity	3294400	718463				

NAME

SECTION

DATE

D.

MAGNUM, INC. AND FOREIGN SUBSIDIARY
Consolidated Statements Workpaper
For the Year Ended December 31, 1992

	Magnum Company	Koala Company	Eliminations Debit	Eliminations Credit	Minority Interest	Consolidated Balances
INCOME STATEMENT						
Sales	545475	189075				
Dividend Income	18876					
Total Revenue	564351	189075				
Cost of Goods Sold	425000	85084				
Other Expenses	50000	33088				
Total Cost and Expense	475000	118172				
Net Income	89351	70903				
Minority Interest in Income	- - -	- - -				
Net Income to Retained Earnings	89351	70903				
RETAINED EARNINGS STATEMENT						
Retained Earnings - 1/1						
Magnum, Inc.	264824					
Koala Company		94450				
Net Income from Above	89351	70903				
Dividends Declared						
Magnum, Inc.	(50000)					
Koala Company		(23595)				
Retained Earnings to						
Balance Sheet - 12/31	304175	141758				

D. (Continued)

BALANCE SHEET	Magnum Company	Koala Company	Eliminations Debit	Eliminations Credit	Minority Interest	Consolidated Balances
Cash	4 0 0 0 0	2 3 6 7 2				
Accounts Receivable	1 2 5 0 0 0	8 0 4 8 4				
Inventory	1 1 5 0 0 0	7 1 0 1 6				
Investment in Koala Company	4 2 5 0 2 5	- -				
Land	5 9 4 0 0	1 4 2 0 3 1				
Buildings and Equipment	2 0 0 0 0 0	1 8 9 3 7 5				
Accumulated Depreciation	(1 2 5 0 0 0)	(7 1 0 1 6)				
Difference between Cost and						
Book Value	- -	- -				
Excess of Cost over Fair Value						
	8 3 9 4 2 5	4 3 5 5 6 2				
Accounts Payable	1 0 2 5 0	4 7 3 4 4				
Notes Payable	2 5 0 0 0	9 4 6 9				
Capital Stock						
Magnum, Inc.	5 0 0 0 0 0					
Koala Company		2 3 6 1 2 5				
Translation Adjustment						
Magnum, Inc.						
Koala Company		8 6 6				
Retained Earnings from Above	3 0 4 1 7 5	1 4 1 7 5 8				
Minority Interest in Net Assets	8 3 9 4 2 5	4 3 5 5 6 2				